SFLEP Biography Titles 英汉对照／外教社人物传记丛书（第二辑）

LANCE ARMSTRONG

兰斯·阿姆斯特朗

Matt Doeden

权 锋 译注

上海外语教育出版社
外教社 SHANGHAI FOREIGN LANGUAGE EDUCATION PRESS

图书在版编目（CIP）数据

兰斯·阿姆斯特朗 / （美）多顿（Doeden，M.）著；
权锋译注. —上海：上海外语教育出版社，2008（2018重印）
（外教社人物传记丛书. 第2辑）
ISBN 978-7-5446-0902-9

Ⅰ.兰… Ⅱ.①多… ②权… Ⅲ.阿姆斯特朗，L.—传记
Ⅳ.K837.125.47

中国版本图书馆CIP数据核字（2008）第104029号

图字：09-2007-688号

图片来源 / 东方IC

出版发行：上海外语教育出版社
（上海外国语大学内） 邮编：200083
电　　话：021-65425300（总机）
电子邮箱：bookinfo@sflep.com.cn
网　　址：http://www.sflep.com.cn　　http://www.sflep.com
责任编辑：徐　喆

印　　刷：上海中华印刷有限公司
开　　本：850×1168　1/32　印张5　字数153千字
版　　次：2008年10月第1版　2018年1月第3次印刷
印　　数：1 000册

书　　号：ISBN 978-7-5446-0902-9 / K·0015
定　　价：20.00元

本版图书如有印装质量问题，可向本社调换

Biography 外教社人物传记丛书

出版前言

曾经有人做了一项调查，拥有最多读者的书籍是传记。阅读一本优秀的人物传记，往往可以使人振作精神，奋发图强，尤其对于青少年，阅读传记更可以使他们建立起正确的人生坐标，从而开拓美好的未来。

上海外语教育出版社从美国乐勒出版集团引进的“外教社人物传记丛书”就是这样一套奉献给青少年朋友的优秀传记丛书。本丛书第一辑13册自2006年初问世以来，得到了广大青年读者的认可和好评。为满足他们了解优秀人物、获取精神财富的需求，我社今年又隆重推出该丛书第二辑13册，包括诺贝尔和平奖获得者德兰修女、曼德拉，政坛风云人物拿破仑、丘吉尔，文学巨匠马克·吐温和简·奥斯丁，天才科学家霍金，影视娱乐界巨星乔治·卢卡斯、克里斯托弗·里夫和奥普拉·温弗瑞，环法自行车赛冠军兰斯·阿姆斯特朗，以及世界历史上著名的两位女王——伊丽莎白一世和克娄巴特拉。阅读这些著名人物的传奇人生，可以帮助青少年朋友们了解西方不同时代的社会历史背景，更能激励他们树立远大理想，以积极的态度直面人生的风雨。

这套传记丛书均由专门从事青少年文学创作的美国资深作家撰写，语言生动活泼，故事性强，引人入胜。外教社特邀一批在翻译方面颇有建树的年轻学者对丛书进行翻译和注释，希望英汉对照加注释这一形式能更好地帮助读者学习英语，享受阅读。

这套丛书特别适合高中生和大学一二年级的学生阅读。我们相信它必将成为青少年朋友们学习英语、探求人生真谛的好伙伴！

上海外语教育出版社

2008年1月

Contents

目　录

PROLOGUE
序言

COMEBACK KID
少年归来

As Lance Armstrong climbed on his bike the morning of July 17, 2001, he looked up at the mountain peaks of the Pyrenees[1] in southern France. The twenty-nine-year-old American cancer survivor had won the Tour de France[2], cycling's greatest race, twice in a row[3]. The grueling[4] race covered more than 3,200 kilometers (1,988 miles) over three weeks. If Lance was going to make it three wins in a row, he had a lot of work to do. Entering stage 10 of a twenty-stage race, Lance was in twenty-third place, more than 35 minutes behind the leader. No Tour cyclist had ever come back to win from so far behind.

Still, Lance and his teammates on the U.S. Postal Service team were confident. The first nine stages of the race had been on mostly flat ground. But the Tour was entering the mountains. Stage 10, an agonizing 209-kilometer (130-mile) climb through the Pyrenees, was exactly the kind of ride Lance could dominate. Many of the riders ahead of him were sprinters[5]—excellent riders on flat ground. But most of them would struggle with the difficult climb of more than 6,000 feet over three mountain peaks.

One of Lance's biggest challengers for the title was Germany's Jan Ullrich. Early in the stage, Lance and his teammates let Ullrich lead the way. They wanted him out in front doing the hardest work. In cycling, riding behind someone is easier than leading because the rear cyclist meets less air resistance—a strategy called drafting. The stage would take more than six hours, and Lance didn't want to wear out his legs too early. Better to let the competition do all the work.

As he rode, Lance used a radio headset[6] to talk to the team coach, Johan Bruyneel. Together, they formed a plan.

2001年7月17日清晨，兰斯·阿姆斯特朗骑上自行车，抬头看了看法国南部的比利牛斯山脉的顶峰。这位29岁的美国癌症康复者曾连续两次赢得最重要的自行车赛事——环法自行车赛——的冠军。这项令人筋疲力尽的赛事历时3个星期，总行程超过3 200公里（1 988英里）。如果兰斯想连续第3次蝉联环法自行车赛的冠军，他还有很多事情要做。环法自行车赛共分20个赛段，在第10赛段，兰斯排名第23位，落后领先者35分钟。还没有哪位参加这项比赛的自行车手落后这么多还赢得了比赛。

但是兰斯和他所在的美国邮政车队的队友却充满信心。环法自行车赛的前9个赛段的比赛大多在平地进行，但比赛即将进入山地赛段。在比利牛斯山脉进行的第10赛段是令选手头痛的长达209公里（130英里）的爬坡赛段，而这正是兰斯能够主宰的比赛。排在兰斯前面的很多都是冲刺型选手——他们是平地赛段的佼佼者，但面对跨越3座6 000多英尺海拔的山峰的爬坡赛段却显得很吃力。

兰斯夺冠道路上最大的竞争对手之一是德国选手扬·乌尔里希。在比赛的前段，兰斯和他的队友让乌尔里希保持领先，故意让他在前面干最苦的差事。在自行车比赛中，骑在其他选手后面的选手因为遇到的风阻更小，所以比骑在前面的选手更为轻松——这就是紧随其后战术。第10赛段历时超过6小时，兰斯可不想他的双腿过早疲劳过度。最好还是通过比赛达到消耗对手的目的。

在骑行中，兰斯通过头戴式受话器与车队教练乔汉·布鲁尼尔交谈。他们共同制定了一个计划：兰斯

[1] the Pyrenees 比利牛斯山脉

[2] Tour de France 环法自行车赛（世界上历史最悠久、规模最大的自行车赛事）

[3] in a row 连续地

[4] grueling 令人筋疲力尽的

[5] sprinters 短距离全速奔跑者

[6] headset （常连送话器的）一幅头戴式受话器

Lance would pretend to be struggling in the ride. He would look tired and beaten. Because he was a two-time champion, he knew the television cameras would be on him. If he looked worn out, Ullrich and the others might attack and push themselves too hard. Lance could ride at the back of the peloton[1], while his rivals did even more work.

Lance did his best acting job. He hung his head. He sent his teammates to bring him extra water bottles. The act fooled everybody. TV broadcasters quickly noticed that the race's defending champion was lagging behind. "It's a long way back to see Armstrong," one announcer said. "He does not look good, and he should not be riding so far down the group; he's obviously having a horrendous[2] day."

At the front of the peloton, Ullrich was among those who fell for the bluff[3]. The leaders attacked hard, standing and pumping the pedals as fast as they could. They wanted to set a pace so fast that Lance would drop, or fall away from the group. If they had a chance to end his hopes of winning a third straight[4] Tour, they were going to take it.

Still, Lance stayed in the back, waiting. He was more than 7 minutes behind Ullrich and the stage leader, Laurent Roux. But that was okay. It was all according to his plan.

Finally, at the foot of a mountain called the Alpe d'Huez, the time came to attack. Lance nodded to his teammates and stomped[5] down on the pedals. They sailed through the peloton, eating up huge chunks of the lead Ullrich and Roux had built. As the road started to ascend into the stage's final climb, Lance sailed around a sharp turn. There, in front of him, was Ullrich. The German was struggling with the climb, exhausted from a day of leading and from his early attack. Lance's bluff had worked—he had fooled his rival into using up his strength too early.

假装精疲力竭，对比赛力不从心。兰斯知道，身为两届环法自行车赛冠军，自己是摄像机追逐的焦点。如果他看起来筋疲力尽，乌尔里希和其他选手可能会冲刺，进而劳累过度。兰斯可以紧随主车群后面，而他的对手比他更加辛苦。

兰斯的演技不错。他耷拉着脑袋，并让队友提供额外的水瓶。他的表演把所有人都骗了。电视播音员们很快注意到卫冕冠军落在了后面。一位播音员说："阿姆斯特朗远远落在后面，看起来状态不佳。他不应该离队伍这么远。很明显，对他来说，今天是非常糟糕的一天。"

在主车群的前部，乌尔里希和其他人一样被假象欺骗了。领先的选手纷纷从车座上站起来，双脚以最快的速度蹬着脚踏板，拼命冲刺起来。他们加快速度，希望兰斯会跟不上他们的速度，或被队伍甩开。他们甘冒风险，只要能打消兰斯想连续第3次夺冠的念头。

兰斯跟在队伍的后面，等待着时机。他比乌尔里希和第10赛段的第一名洛朗·鲁落后7分多钟。不过还好，一切都在兰斯计划之中。

最终，在一座名叫阿尔贝杜埃的山的山脚下，兰斯开始加速冲刺。向队友点头示意后，他开始用力踩脚踏板。他和队友穿越了主车群，大大缩短了与乌尔里希和洛朗·鲁的差距。随着道路越来越陡峭，比赛进入最后的爬坡路段，兰斯快速转过一个弯道。前面就是乌尔里希。由于一整天都骑在队伍前部，而且过早就开始冲刺，这位德国选手爬坡非常吃力。兰斯的骗局奏效了——他愚弄了对手，使其过早就消耗完了体力。

[1] peloton （法语）自行车比赛中的主车群

[2] horrendous 可怕的

[3] bluff 虚张声势

[4] straight 连续的

[5] stomped 重踩，重踏

"Armstrong has maybe been playing an incredible poker game today by sitting at the back and letting everybody else do the work," said a TV broadcaster.

As Lance sped by Ullrich, he looked back over his shoulder. He wanted to see the expression on the German's face—wanted to know whether Ullrich was truly beaten. He got his answer quickly. Lance surged[1] forward again to see if his rival could keep up. He couldn't. Soon, Lance passed Roux as well and sailed to the finish line, almost a full 2 minutes ahead of Ullrich. He shook his arms in the air and hopped off the bike.

Lance was back in the race. But in the overall standings[2], he still trailed France's François Simon by 20 minutes. He hoped his furious attack hadn't left him too tired for the next day. Stage 11 was another tough climb, this time a 32-kilometer (20-mile) time trial[3]. A time trial stage is different from a regular stage. Riders don't all leave the starting line at the same time. They start spaced 3 minutes apart. They cannot rely on their teammates and drafting. They have to do the work on their own.

Again, Lance was measuring himself against Jan Ullrich, who started before him. As Lance crossed each checkpoint, his coach told him his times. He was faster than Ullrich—a lot faster. With about 4 kilometers (2.5 miles) to go, he was ahead of the German by 42 seconds. He pushed hard toward the finish line and crossed with a time of 1 hour, 7 minutes, 27 seconds, a full minute faster than Ullrich, who finished second. The climb pulled Lance to within 13 minutes of the lead[4], still held by Simon.

Lance kept up the fierce pace. He cut the lead to 9:10 in stage 12, then made his big move during the 194-kilometer (120.5-mile) stage 13. He and Ullrich both rode at

一位电视播音员说："阿姆斯特朗今天像是打了一场精彩的扑克牌比赛。他跟在队伍后面，让其他选手替他减小空气阻力。"

当兰斯快速超过乌尔里希时，他扭头看了看。他想看看这位德国选手脸上的表情——想确定乌尔里希是否真的被击败了。兰斯很快得到了答案。兰斯再次加速冲刺，想看看他的对手能否跟上。乌尔里希跟不上。很快，兰斯又超过了鲁，快速冲过了终点线，几乎比乌尔里希提前整整2分钟。兰斯向空中挥了挥手臂，一跃跳下了他的自行车。

兰斯又回来了。但是他的总排名依然比法国的弗朗索瓦·西蒙落后20分钟。他希望自己没有因为今天的急速冲刺而劳累过度，无法应付第2天的比赛。第11赛段是另一个艰苦的长达32公里（20英里）的爬坡计时赛。计时赛段与常规赛段不同。计时赛中选手不是同时出发，而是每隔3分钟一名选手出发。选手无法依靠队友，也无法使用紧随前车的战术，而只能依靠自己。

兰斯依然把竞争对手锁定为比他提前出发的扬·乌尔里希。每当兰斯经过一个检查站，他的教练就会告诉他他目前的比赛情况。他比乌尔里希快——快得多。赛段还剩4公里（2.5英里）的时候，他领先这个德国人42秒。他快速骑向终点线，以1小时7分27秒的成绩结束比赛，比第2名乌尔里希快了整整1分钟。在这个爬坡赛段，兰斯与比赛总成绩领先者西蒙之间的差距缩短到13分钟以内。

兰斯保持着高速度。在第12赛段，他把与领先者的差距缩短到9分10秒。在长达194公里（120.5英里）的第13赛段，兰斯开始发挥最大的实力。这个赛段比赛的大部分时间里，他和乌尔里希都骑在前面。

[1] surged 猛冲

[2] standings （根据运动队或运动员历次比赛成绩排列的）名次表

[3] time trial （汽车比赛等的）计时赛

[4] lead 领先程度

the front for most of the stage. Before the last of six climbs, Lance attacked hard. Ullrich couldn't keep up. Again, the German had to watch Lance pull away[1] and win another mountain stage. Lance blew away[2] the whole field and took over the yellow jersey, the cycling shirt worn by the leader of the Tour de France. In only four stages of racing, Lance had made the biggest comeback in Tour history—he'd gone from 35 minutes behind to more than 3 minutes ahead.

He seemed unstoppable. Ullrich, badly beaten again, was discouraged. "I tried everything that was possible," he said. "I have to wait for a black[3] day for Armstrong, otherwise he is unbeatable."

Ullrich feared what most of the other riders knew. With a 3-minute lead, only a disaster would stop Lance Armstrong. No disaster came. Lance won one more stage, the eighteenth, and cruised into Paris for the final stage with a 6-minute win over second-place Ullrich. After more than eighty-six hours on the bike, Lance was the champion—for the third year in a row.

"It's the best feeling," Lance said. "As always, I am happy to finally arrive, to finally finish the Tour. It's a special feeling."

[1] pull away　摆脱；逃离

[2] blew away　（比赛中）大败

[3] black　倒霉的；不祥的

在最后6个坡道，兰斯急速冲刺。乌尔里希无法跟上。这位德国选手不得不再次看着对方超过自己，又赢下一个山地赛段。兰斯击败了所有对手，夺取了黄色领骑衫——环法自行车赛总成绩领先者穿的比赛服。仅仅通过4个赛段，兰斯就创造了环法自行车赛历史上最大的反超——从落后35分钟到领先3分多钟。

兰斯显得不可阻挡。又一次彻底失败的乌尔里希感到气馁。他说："我试了所有的方法。我只能希望他哪天不走运，否则他是不可战胜的。"

乌尔里希的担忧也正是其他大多数选手的担忧。只有灾难能够阻止拥有3分钟领先优势的兰斯·阿姆斯特朗夺冠。没有灾难发生。兰斯又赢下第18赛段，以领先第2名乌尔里希6分钟的优势，昂首挺进最后的巴黎赛段。在自行车上拼搏了超过86小时之后，兰斯成为了冠军——也是三连冠。

兰斯说："这种感觉棒极了。和往常一样，我非常高兴最终到达目的地完成比赛。这种感觉很特别。"

CHAPTER ONE

HUMBLE BEGINNINGS

出身贫寒

Lance Armstrong started his life as the baby only one person wanted. His father didn't really want a baby. His mother's mother didn't want her teenage daughter to have a baby. The only person who truly wanted the healthy baby boy was his mother, Linda Gayle Mooneyham.

Linda was just a high school student in Dallas, Texas, when she found out she was pregnant with Lance. At first, she tried to hide her pregnancy with baggy clothing. But soon, it was impossible to hide. Many of her friends and family tried to convince her to give up the baby for adoption[1]. She was too young, they thought, to be raising a child.

But Linda had different ideas. She was going to start a family, and the first step was marrying the baby's father, Eddie Gunderson. Marriage wasn't what Gunderson wanted, but he went along with the plan. The couple lived in a small apartment. Linda's mom, who still didn't support her daughter's decision, almost never came to help. Linda and Eddie took part-time jobs and did what they could to make ends meet[2]. They even worked together on a paper route.

On September 18, 1971, Linda gave birth to a 9-pound, 12-ounce baby boy. She was thrilled. She named the boy Lance after her favorite football player, a wide receiver[3] for the Dallas Cowboys named Lance Rentzel. The childbirth was difficult for Linda, though. She developed a high fever after giving birth. Nurses took care of the baby while she recovered. Almost two days passed before she was able to hold and spend time with little Lance.

Things didn't get any easier when she got the baby back home. Eddie wasn't ready for the responsibility of fatherhood. In his frustration, he sometimes lashed out[4] at Linda. He often left her alone with the baby. For support,

兰斯·阿姆斯特朗刚出生时，只有一个人想要他。他父亲不想要孩子。他外祖母不想她未成年的女儿早为人母。只有一个人真正想要兰斯这个健康的男婴，她就是兰斯的母亲琳达·盖尔·穆尼罕姆。

当琳达发现怀上兰斯的时候，她还只是得克萨斯州达拉斯的一个高中生。起初她穿宽大的衣服来掩盖怀孕的事实。但很快，秘密藏不住了。她的朋友和家人大多劝她放弃这个孩子，由别人来收养。他们认为她还太小，无力抚养孩子。

[1] adoption 收养

但琳达不这么想。她打算建立起一个家庭，而第一步就是嫁给孩子的父亲——埃迪·冈德森。冈德森并不想结婚，但还是同意了琳达的计划。这对新人住在一套小公寓里。琳达的母亲不支持女儿的决定，几乎从未为他们提供帮助。琳达和埃迪做兼职，竭尽全力使收支平衡。他们甚至一起送报纸。

[2] make ends meet 使收支平衡

1971年9月18日，琳达生下了一个9磅12盎司重的男婴。她高兴极了。她以她最喜欢的美式足球运动员——达拉斯牛仔队的外接手兰斯·让泽尔——的名字为男婴取名兰斯。而生产过程却很困难。琳达产后发高烧。在她康复期间，由护士照看着婴儿。产后差不多两天她才能抱着小兰斯，和他呆上一会儿。

[3] wide receiver (美式橄榄球中的)外接手

她带着孩子回家后，情况没有任何好转。埃迪还没有准备好承担为人父者的责任。有时绝望的他会痛打琳达，而且经常让琳达独自照顾

[4] lashed out 猛击

Linda turned to her father, Paul Mooneyham, who was divorced from her mother. Eventually, Linda left Eddie and moved in with her father full-time. Eddie begged her to come back, but Linda knew their relationship was over.

Life with her father was better for Linda and Lance. Father and daughter worked together to care for the baby. Linda watched the baby at night while Paul worked. Paul watched Lance during the day while Linda searched for a job.

Soon, Linda and Lance moved out. They got a small apartment in Oak Cliff, Texas, near Dallas. While she finished high school, Linda worked part-time at a Kentucky Fried Chicken on the corner. She also worked at a small grocery store. She later found a job at the local post office. The jobs didn't pay much, but the little family got by. "All I did, my life, was going to work and raising my son, and I was happy to do it," Linda said.

Trying to earn enough money and still care for Lance was hard on Linda, but she remembers plenty of good times. She loved to read to little Lance. They danced together. She took him on walks, and they went swimming. Lance was in a hurry to keep up with his mother. He started walking when he was only nine months old.

Lance was just a toddler[1] when he had his first fall on a bicycle. Linda and Eddie had divorced, but Eddie still got to visit his son. Once, Eddie wanted to take Lance for a bike ride. As Eddie pedaled, he thought Lance was holding on tight behind him. But the little boy took a nasty[2] fall off the bike. Eddie had to rush him to the hospital for stitches[3]. Linda was furious. She believed that Eddie had proven he couldn't be a good father. Linda told him he couldn't visit Lance anymore.

When Lance was three, Linda found a job as a

孩子。琳达向与她母亲离婚的父亲保罗·穆尼罕姆求助。最后，琳达离开了埃迪，搬到父亲那里住。埃迪求琳达搬回来，但她知道他们的关系走到了尽头。

和父亲住在一起，琳达和兰斯的生活好过些了。琳达与父亲一起照顾孩子。晚上保罗工作的时候琳达照看孩子，白天琳达出去找工作的时候由保罗照看孩子。

很快，琳达和兰斯搬了出去，住在得克萨斯州离达拉斯不远的橡树崖镇的一套小公寓里。琳达完成高中学业后，在街角的肯德基餐厅做兼职，同时在一家小杂货店上班。后来她在当地的邮局找到一份工作，虽然工资不高，但足够她的小家庭所需。琳达说："我一生所做的，就是去工作和抚养我的儿子。我很高兴做这一切。"

琳达很辛苦，既要努力去挣到足够的钱，又要照顾兰斯，但她也有很多美好时光。她喜欢读书给小兰斯听，他俩还一起跳舞、散步、游泳。兰斯急切地想赶上妈妈。他9个月大就开始走路了。

兰斯第一次从自行车上摔下来时，还在蹒跚学步。琳达和埃迪已经离婚，但埃迪有时会来看看孩子。一次，埃迪想骑自行车带兰斯出去。埃迪在骑车，以为后面的兰斯紧紧抓着他，但小兰斯重重地从车上摔了下来。埃迪急忙把他送到医院缝伤口。琳达非常生气，她认定埃迪已经证明自己做不了一个好父亲，因此告诉他以后不准再来看望兰斯。

兰斯3岁的时候，琳达找到了一份秘书工

[1] toddler 学步的小孩；蹒跚行走者

[2] nasty 严重的

[3] stitches （医生在伤口上缝合的）一针

secretary and moved to Richardson, Texas, a suburb of Dallas. She also had a new man in her life, a salesman named Terry Armstrong, whom she married. In time, Terry adopted Lance as his own son, and Lance took on Terry's last name.

Armstrong tried to be a good father to Lance, but he was often misguided. He used a paddle[1] to punish the boy, even for small misbehaviors. He also treated Linda poorly. But he helped pay for everything the family needed, and financial security was important to Linda. She no longer had to worry about having enough money to provide for Lance.

Across the street from Lance's home in Richardson was a store called the Richardson Bike Mart. Jim Hoyt, the owner of the store, often saw Linda and Lance together. He admired how hard Linda worked to raise her son and thought Lance was a fine young boy. When Lance was seven, Hoyt gave Linda a great deal on Lance's first bike. It was a brown Schwinn Mag Scrambler, a BMX model with yellow wheels. Lance loved the bike. To him, the bike represented a freedom he'd never had before. He rode it whenever he could.

When Lance was twelve, the family moved to a new house in Plano, Texas, north of Dallas. Lance was growing up to be a strong boy. He spent hours playing baseball and football. Football is a favorite sport in Texas. It's how young men make a name for themselves, and Lance was eager to prove himself. Despite his strength and athletic ability, Lance had no real talent for football and quickly gave up on the sport.

But he didn't give up on being an athlete. He wanted to compete—and win. Lance learned about a distance-running race held by his school. He had no formal experience in distance running, but he insisted on entering the

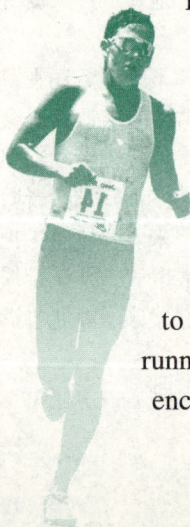

作，并搬到了得克萨斯州的理查德森，这是达拉斯的一个郊区。她遇到了她生命中的另一个男人——一个名叫特里·阿姆斯特朗的销售员，并嫁给了他。最后，特里收养了兰斯，兰斯随了他的姓。

阿姆斯特朗努力成为一个好父亲，但经常受误导。他用短桨体罚兰斯，即使兰斯只是犯了点小错误。他对琳达也不好。但是他帮着负担家里的一切所需，而经济保障对琳达而言非常重要，她不必再为挣足够的钱来供养兰斯而发愁了。

[1] paddle （短而阔的）桨；桨状物

兰斯在理查德森的家的街对面，有一家叫做"理查德森自行车市场"的商店。店主吉姆·霍伊特经常看到琳达和兰斯在一起。他很敬佩琳达努力工作抚养儿子，觉得兰斯是个不错的小男孩。在兰斯7岁的时候，他以非常优惠的价格卖给琳达一辆自行车，也就是兰斯的第一辆自行车。这是一辆棕色的施温牌BMX型号山地车，车轮是黄色的。兰斯非常喜欢这辆车，因为它代表着一种他从未拥有过的自由。他一有机会就骑着它。

兰斯12岁的时候，他家搬到了达拉斯北边的得克萨斯州普莱诺的一个新房子里。兰斯渐渐长成了一个强壮的男孩，棒球和美式足球一玩就是几小时。美式足球在得克萨斯州非常受欢迎，年轻人靠它出名。兰斯急于想证明自己，尽管他很强壮，也有运动才能，但在美式足球方面并没有天赋，于是很快就放弃了这项运动。

但他并没有放弃成为一名运动员，他渴望比赛——并赢得比赛。兰斯得知学校举办长跑比赛，尽管没有关于这项运动的正式经验，他还是坚持要参加。他告诉母亲他会赢。他兑现了承诺，

race. He told his mother he was going to win. He came through on the promise, one of his first tastes of victory in a race. The win was especially sweet because Lance beat many boys who were star football players. He proved to himself that he was a good athlete too.

Some of Lance's friends had joined a community swimming club, and he wanted to try swimming as well. At first, his attempts to swim looked like a disaster. He flopped[1] into the water with no idea what to do. Although he was twelve years old, he had to take swimming classes with kids almost half his age. But as bad as he was at first, he worked hard to improve.

Chris MacCurdy, a coach at the swimming club, saw that Lance worked hard and had a lot of stamina[2]. MacCurdy worked with Lance on his technique. Something must have clicked, because this help quickly turned Lance into one of the club's best swimmers. By age thirteen, he was one of the top swimmers in Texas in his age group. He swam in the 1,500-meter freestyle, a race in which swimmers are free to use any swimming stroke[3] they wish.

A problem soon developed with Lance's newest passion. The swimming club was about 10 miles from his home, but often his mother was busy working and couldn't drive him to practice. He wasn't about to let this stop him, though. He would climb on his bike and ride the 10 miles to the club, swim for several hours, then ride home again. It was a grueling schedule, but Lance didn't complain. If that was what he had to do to compete, then that was what he'd do.

而这也是他最初得到的几个比赛胜利之一。胜利的感觉很好，因为很多被他击败的年轻小伙是美式足球明星运动员。他证明了自己也是个优秀的运动员。

兰斯的一些朋友加入了一家社区游泳俱乐部，他也想尝试一下游泳。起先，他游得非常糟糕，一跳进水里就不知道该怎么办。他已经12岁了，但还要和年龄比他小一半的孩子一起参加游泳学习班。尽管一开始表现很差，但他勤奋练习。

游泳俱乐部教练克里斯·麦克科迪看到兰斯很勤奋，也很有耐力，就帮助兰斯提高游泳技巧。他俩很合得来，很快兰斯就成了俱乐部最好的游泳者之一。到了13岁的时候，兰斯已经是得克萨斯州他这个年龄组最好的游泳者之一了，他的项目是1 500米自由泳，自由泳是游泳者任意选择泳姿的游泳项目。

兰斯对游泳很着迷，但很快就有问题出现了：游泳俱乐部离家大约10英里，而他妈妈经常因忙于工作而无法开车送他去练习。尽管如此，兰斯不想因为这个原因而放弃。他骑车10英里到俱乐部，练几小时游泳，再骑车回家。这样的安排令人筋疲力尽，但兰斯从未抱怨。如果为了比赛就得这么做，那他就愿意这么做。

[1] flopped （扑通一声）沉重地落下

[2] stamina 耐力；精力

[3] stroke 游泳姿势

CHAPTER TWO

JUNIOR

少年兰斯

By age thirteen, Lance had proven himself to be a good runner and an excellent swimmer. He was always on his bike, pedaling away. So when he saw an advertisement for a junior triathlon[1] called IronKids, it seemed like a perfect fit.

A triathlon is a race with three parts. Competitors begin the race with a swim, then climb onto bikes for a long ride. At the end of the ride, the racers jump off their bikes and begin a distance run. Triathlon is an exhausting sport for which few people are suited. But it was perfect for Lance. Excited, he told his mother about the race. Linda, who was beginning to think Lance might have a future as an athlete, shared his enthusiasm. The two went out and bought a multispeed racing bike called a Mercier for the race.

Lance hadn't ever raced in or even seen a triathlon before. He hadn't done any special training for the race. But that didn't slow him down. He started off strong in the swimming part and was one of the first racers out of the water. In the second part, the cycling, he pulled out to a big lead. When he finished that part of the race, he jumped off the bike and put on running shoes. He took off toward the finish line with nobody else in sight. He easily won the race, blowing away all his competition. A few weeks later, he won a second junior triathlon in Houston, Texas.

Lance was hooked[2]. The triathlon combined three of his favorite sports. It required great endurance and determination, and he had both. Unlike many competitors, Lance didn't mind the pain in his muscles during a race. He would later write, "If it was a sufferfest, I was good at it."

While Lance was proving himself to be one of the

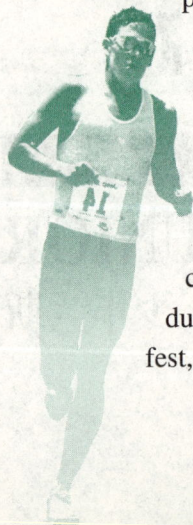

[1] triathlon 三项全能运动

[2] hooked <喻> 引（人）上钩

13岁的兰斯已经证明自己是个不错的跑步运动员和优秀的游泳选手。他总是骑着他的自行车。因此当他看到一个名叫"钢铁少年"的青少年三项全能比赛的广告时，觉得自己非常适合。

三项全能比赛包含3部分：选手们刚开始进行游泳比赛，然后是长距离的自行车比赛，最后是长跑比赛。三项全能比赛非常辛苦，适合从事这种项目的人不多，但兰斯非常适合。兴奋的兰斯告诉妈妈他要参赛，而琳达也开始觉得兰斯做运动员可能会有前途，所以也很兴奋。他们俩出去买了一辆比赛用的梅西尔牌变速自行车。

兰斯没参加过三项全能比赛，甚至以前从未看过这种比赛。赛前他没有针对比赛进行过任何特殊训练，但他的表现并不差：游泳比赛一开始就表现很好，是首先完成游泳比赛的几个选手之一；在比赛的第2段即自行车比赛中，他领先了其他选手很多；自行车比赛一结束他就穿上跑鞋，向比赛终点跑去，这个时候他的视线里没有出现任何对手。他击败所有对手，轻松赢得比赛。几个星期后，他在得克萨斯州的休斯敦又赢得了第2个青少年三项全能比赛的胜利。

兰斯迷上了三项全能比赛，因为它把他最喜欢的3个运动项目结合在一起。三项全能比赛要求运动员有极强的耐力和意志，而他两者兼备。与很多选手不同，兰斯不在乎比赛时的肌肉疼痛。他后来写道："如果说它是受苦的节日，那我非常善于此道。"

尽管兰斯正在证明自己是州里顶尖的青少年

state's top young athletes, his home life wasn't happy. His stepfather was becoming a bigger problem. Terry Armstrong didn't treat Linda with respect. He punished Lance too severely. Lance once ran away from home after a fight with Terry and didn't come back until the next day. Soon, Linda left her husband. Once again, Lance was all she had, and she was all he had. But he was old enough to help his mother. He did chores around the house. He was also earning his own money by winning triathlons.

Even though he was just fifteen, Lance wanted to test his skills against the best adults. He entered the 1987 President's Triathlon in Lake Lavon, Texas. Nobody expected a teenage kid to keep up with the large field of experienced adult athletes. But he held his own, finishing thirty-second.

He entered more adult triathlons and started winning some of them. Soon, his name was becoming known. The adults called him Junior and marveled at how a boy could beat so many grown men. *Triathlete* magazine named him the national Rookie[1] of the Year in sprint triathlons. The magazine said he was one of the greatest athletes the sport had ever seen. He was a rising star. And he was making good prize money[2]—about $20,000 a year—by age sixteen.

The biking segments of the triathlon quickly became Lance's strength. He worked hard on his cycling and started entering bike races called criteriums, or crits. These popular races featured some of the best riders in Texas. Lance joined a racing team sponsored by Jim Hoyt (the bicycle shop owner who had helped Lance get his first bike) and the Richardson Bike Mart. Lance quickly moved up from crits for beginners to races for the most skilled riders. He also continued to compete in triathlons.

运动员之一，但他的家庭生活并不幸福。他的继父特里·阿姆斯特朗越来越成问题：不尊重琳达而且惩罚兰斯过重。有一次兰斯和特里打了一架后离家出走，第2天才回来。不久，琳达离开了丈夫。兰斯和妈妈再一次成为对方拥有的全部。但兰斯已经长大，可以帮助妈妈了。他在家做家务，还参加三项全能比赛赢取奖金。

尽管只有15岁，兰斯却想挑战最优秀的成人运动员来验证自己的技能。他参加了1987年在得克萨斯州拉文湖举行的总统杯三项全能比赛。没人指望一个少年能跟上巨大的赛场中富有经验的成人运动员，但他坚持完成了比赛，获得第32名。

他参加的成人三项全能比赛越来越多，而且开始赢得其中的一些比赛。不久他就出名了。那些成人运动员叫他“小不点”，他们很吃惊一个男孩子竟能击败这么多成年男子。《三项全能运动员》杂志评选他为全国短距离三项全能运动的年度最佳新人，并评价说他是该项运动有史以来最伟大的运动员之一。他是一颗冉冉升起的新星，而且到16岁时，他开始赢得可观的比赛奖金——差不多一年2万美元。

三项全能比赛中的自行车比赛很快成了兰斯的强项。他苦练自行车项目，并开始参加名为绕圈赛的自行车比赛。这些比赛很受欢迎，而且有得克萨斯州一些最好的自行车选手参加。兰斯参加了由吉姆·霍伊特（帮助兰斯买第一辆自行车的自行车店店主）和“理查德森自行车市场”赞助的自行车队。兰斯很快就从针对新人的绕圈赛转到了顶尖好手参加的比赛，同时他还参加三项全能比赛。

[1] Rookie　新手；新兵

[2] prize money　奖金

By this time, Lance was attending classes at Plano East High School. School was never his main priority[1], though. He was always on his bike, pedaling mile after mile. He would ride all the way into Dallas. He was strong and confident — sometimes too confident. He would ride in Dallas's heavy traffic, dodging[2] cars and running through stoplights. One time, his overconfidence got him into serious trouble. He ran through a stoplight and got hit by a truck. The impact threw Lance from the bike onto the street. He wasn't wearing a helmet. He smashed his head against the street and got a big gash[3] on his foot. An ambulance took him to the hospital. His bike was ruined.

Lance's doctors put some stitches in his head and his foot and told him he wouldn't be able to race for a while. But Lance didn't want to hear that. His next triathlon was less than a week away. He borrowed a friend's bike and entered the race anyway, despite the painful wound on his foot. Lance's doctor was later shocked to learn that his young patient had ignored the pain and finished third in the event.

As Lance continued to train, he felt more and more comfortable on the bike. Soon, dreams of being a professional road racer replaced his dreams of being a star in the triathlon.

In September 1989, during his last year of high school, Lance entered a 12-mile time trial in Moriarty, New Mexico. Because each rider starts separately in a time trial, Lance would be competing only against the clock. The course was flat and easy to ride, which meant that many riders could score their best times. Lance knew a good time would impress people in the cycling world. He needed to be in top form[4].

But when Lance arrived at the time trial, he realized he'd made a mistake. He hadn't planned on cold weather. He had only his normal cycling clothes. As he prepared

这个时候兰斯还在普莱诺东部高中读书，但读书从来不是他的主要目标。他总是骑着自行车，不停地骑着。他会一直骑到达拉斯。他很强壮，也很自信——有时太过自信了。他在达拉斯拥挤的车流中骑车，避开汽车，还闯红灯。有一次他的过分自信使他惹上了大麻烦：他闯红灯时被卡车给撞了。撞击的冲击力把他从自行车上甩到了马路上，他没戴头盔，头撞在了马路上，脚上划了个大伤口。他被救护车送往医院。他的自行车报废了。

医生缝合了兰斯头上和脚上的伤口，告诫他有一段时间不能参加比赛。但兰斯并不想听这些。不到一个星期，他的下一个三项全能比赛就开始了。他借了朋友的自行车，不管脚上的伤痛还是参赛了。后来得知这位年轻的病人不顾伤痛，以第3名的成绩完成了比赛，兰斯的医生十分震惊。

兰斯在训练中越来越喜欢在自行车上的感觉。很快，他开始梦想成为一名职业公路自行车赛选手，而不再是成为一名三项全能明星。

1989年9月，兰斯在高中的最后一年参加了在新墨西哥州莫里亚蒂市举行的一个12英里计时赛。计时赛中每个选手都是单独出发，因此兰斯比赛的对手就是时间。路段很平，易于骑行，很多选手都可以取得自己最好的成绩。兰斯清楚，取得好成绩可以使自行车运动的圈内人士注意到自己。他需要展现出最好的竞技状态。

但当兰斯抵达比赛现场时，他意识到自己犯了个错误。他对寒冷天气没有准备，只穿了平常的自行车比赛服。他在寒冷的早

[1] priority 优先考虑的事

[2] dodging 躲避；闪开

[3] gash （深长的）划开的伤口

[4] in top form （运动员等的）竞技状态极好

for the race in the chilly[1] morning air, he couldn't get warmed up. He knew he wouldn't do well in the time trial if he started out cold. He ran to find his mom. Linda had only a small pink jacket. Lance was far too big for the jacket, but he put it on anyway. He turned up the heat in his mom's car and tried his best to stay warm. When it was finally time to start, Lance climbed out of the car and onto the bike. Despite his earlier fears, Lance was on top of his game. He didn't just do well in the time trial—he broke the course record by an amazing 45 seconds.

Lance's cycling career was off to a great start. The U.S. Cycling Federation, a national association for bicycle racers, had learned about his performance at Moriarty. Federation officials asked Lance to join the U.S. junior cycling team and go to Moscow, Russia, for the 1990 Junior World Championships. The chance to join the team and compete overseas was huge. Lance excitedly told administrators at his school that he needed to be excused from classes to take part. But the school officials weren't impressed. They told Lance he didn't have permission to miss class.

Lance went anyway. He started by training with the team in Colorado. Then he flew to Moscow for the race, a time trial. Lance started with a bang. His first few laps around the course were the fastest in the field. But he tired out by the end and had a disappointing finish. Even so, the newcomer had impressed many cycling experts. They thought that with the proper coaching, Lance had the tools to become a very exciting cyclist.

Lance came home feeling good about himself, but those good feelings quickly disappeared. He learned that because he had left school without permission, he wouldn't be able to graduate. Linda found a small private school

[1] chilly　寒冷的

晨为比赛做准备活动，发现无法热身。他知道如果身体还没有热起来就出发，他就不可能在计时赛中取得好成绩。他跑去找妈妈。琳达只穿了一件很小的粉红色夹克，夹克太小，但他还是穿上了。他把母亲汽车里的暖气开大，想尽办法保暖。当比赛最终快要开始时，兰斯走出汽车，跨上了自行车。尽管兰斯先前有些担心，但比赛还是尽在他的掌握。他不仅在计时赛中表现良好——他还打破了比赛纪录，新纪录比旧纪录快了45秒，令人惊奇。

兰斯的自行车生涯取得了良好的开端。美国自行车协会——一个全国性的自行车选手组织，得知了他在莫里亚蒂市的表现，于是协会官员邀请兰斯加入美国青少年自行车队，参加1990年在莫斯科举办的世界青少年冠军赛。能够加入这样一支队伍，并征战海外，这个机会实在太难得了，兴奋的兰斯告诉他所在高中的管理者他想请假参赛。但学校官员不为所动，他们告诉兰斯他不准缺课。

兰斯还是去参赛了。开始他在科罗拉多随队训练，然后他飞往莫斯科参加比赛，项目是计时赛。兰斯有一个良好的开端，刚开始几圈他是赛场中最快的。但比赛末尾由于疲劳，他慢下来，最终比赛成绩令人失望。即使这样，他这个新手还是给很多自行车比赛专家留下了深刻印象。专家们认为，如果调教得当，兰斯具备成为一名优秀自行车手的才能。

兰斯自我感觉良好地回到家，但他的好心情很快消失了。他得知由于他未经允许离校，他将不能毕业。琳达找到一家名叫“弯曲橡

called Bending Oaks that would allow Lance to graduate if he finished a few courses. He didn't graduate with his old classmates, but Lance still got his diploma. He was ready to leave home and start a full-time career as a cyclist.

树”的小型私立学校，在这里兰斯完成几门课程就可以毕业。兰斯没有和他的老同学一起毕业，但他还是拿到了毕业文凭。他已经准备离家，要成为一名职业自行车手。

CHAPTER THREE

GROWING PAINS

成长的痛苦

In 1990 Lance moved out on his own. He settled in Austin, Texas, where he rented an apartment. He also joined the U.S. national cycling team under coach Chris Carmichael. Carmichael saw that the eighteen-year-old Texan was a powerful rider with enormous potential. But he also saw a young man who was stubborn and hadn't had much coaching. Lance wanted to ride at full blast[1] all the time. He didn't understand the strategy of holding a little energy in reserve.

Lance's first race for the team was the 1990 Amateur World Championship in Japan. The race, held on a very hot day, was 115 miles long, with a difficult uphill section. Carmichael wanted Lance to draft—to stay behind other riders and save some energy for the end of the race.

But Lance didn't listen to his coach. He was overconfident and quickly pedaled to a big lead. The lead grew and grew to almost 90 seconds, but Lance was exhausting himself. He got tired and slowed down. His lead fell to a minute, then to 30 seconds. Soon the peloton had caught him. Lance couldn't mount[2] a charge at the end. He could only slide back into the draft and finish eleventh. It was a disappointing finish after the fast start. But despite the mistake, Lance's time was the fastest by an American rider in more than fifteen years.

Impatience wasn't Lance's only problem during races. His aggressive style also got him into trouble. He didn't give his opponents any respect. He would shout at them and insult them during races. He wouldn't work with his own teammates. He would show them up[3], just to prove that he was better. In response, other riders sometimes got in his way on purpose[4] and tried to slow him down. They refused to draft with him. By

1990年，兰斯从家里搬了出去，在得克萨斯州的奥斯丁租了一套公寓，并定居下来。他还加入了美国国家自行车队，教练是克里斯·卡米卡尔。卡米卡尔看出这个18岁的得州人强壮有力，前途无限，但也看出他倔强固执，没受过什么训练。兰斯任何时候都一味全速前进，不理解保存体力的战术。

兰斯随队参加的第一场比赛是1990年在日本举办的世界业余冠军赛。比赛全长115英里，包含一段困难的爬坡赛段，比赛当天天气异常炎热。卡米卡尔让兰斯“搭顺风车”——骑在其他车手后面，为后面的比赛节省些体力。

但过于自信的兰斯不听教练的话，他快速蹬着脚踏板，很快领先其他选手一大截。兰斯的领先优势不断扩大到差不多90秒，但他逐渐耗尽了体力，由于疲劳而减速了。他的领先优势逐渐缩短到1分钟，然后是30秒，很快主车群赶上了他。在比赛末尾他无力冲刺，只能骑在其他选手后面，最终以第11名的成绩完成了比赛。虽然一开始他速度很快，但最终的比赛成绩却令人失望。尽管有这样的失误，兰斯的成绩依然是15多年当中美国车手的最好成绩。

比赛中缺乏耐心不是兰斯唯一的问题。他富于攻击性的风格也使他陷入麻烦：他不尊重对手，在比赛中对他们大喊大叫，侮辱他们；他不愿意与自己的队友合作，并会使他们难堪，以此显示自己是最棒的。作为回应，其他选手有时会故意挡他的路，想使他慢下来；他们还拒绝

[1] at full blast　全力以赴地；以最快的速度

[2] mount　发动

[3] show them up　使难堪

[4] on purpose　故意地

being selfish, Lance was isolating himself.

Lance didn't like the idea, common in team racing, that one racer should move over to let another one win. This situation came into focus in a race in Italy shortly after the 1990 Amateur Worlds. Lance was riding as an amateur on the U.S. cycling team (amateur cyclists get paid, but they can't win prize money at international events). He had also signed on with a professional team called Subaru-Montgomery. Both teams were competing in the race.

The race was held over ten stages, each on a different day. As the race went on, only one rider, an American named Nate Reese, was ahead of Lance. One evening between stages, Eddie Borysewicz, the coach of the Subaru-Montgomery team, told Lance that he was expected to help Reese, a professional, win the race.

Lance didn't know what to do. He wasn't used to the idea of staying back to let somebody else win. He talked to Coach Carmichael about it. His coach told him to ignore Borysewicz. If Lance had a chance to win, Carmichael said, he had to take it. Lance also phoned Linda back in Texas. She agreed with Carmichael. Lance had to ride the best he could.

Lance followed Carmichael's advice. In the next stage, he pushed hard to take over the lead. His fast pace left Reese far behind. This decision made Lance very unpopular with the professionals on the Subaru-Montgomery team, and he knew it would cost him his spot on the team. In addition, the Italian fans were angry that an American was leading the race. They threw glass and tacks[1] onto the road, hoping to make Lance blow a tire.

It didn't matter, though. Lance crossed the finish line first, with a margin of victory of more than a minute. It

让他“搭顺风车”。由于自私，兰斯越来越孤立。

让其他选手赢得比赛的做法，在自行车队比赛中很常见，而兰斯对此却很厌恶。1990年世界业余冠军赛后不久，在一次在意大利举行的比赛中，这个问题成了焦点。在这次比赛中，兰斯作为美国自行车队的一名业余选手参赛（业余选手有报酬，但他们不能在国际比赛中赢取奖金），同时他也是一家名叫苏巴鲁—蒙哥马利的职业车队的签约车手。这两支队伍都参加了这场比赛。

比赛包含10个赛段，一天进行一个赛段的比赛。随着比赛的进行，只有一个选手，一个名叫内特·里斯的美国人领先于兰斯。两场比赛之间的一个晚上，埃迪·博里塞维茨——苏巴鲁—蒙哥马利车队的教练——告诉兰斯，他希望兰斯能帮职业车手里斯赢得比赛。

兰斯不知所措。他不习惯呆在后面，而让别人获胜。他告诉了教练卡米卡尔这件事情。卡米卡尔告诉他别听博里塞维茨的话，他还说如果有获胜的机会，就必须抓住它。兰斯还给远在得克萨斯的琳达打了电话。琳达同意卡米卡尔的意见。兰斯必须对比赛全力以赴。

兰斯听从卡米卡尔的建议，在下一个赛段他尽力冲刺，获得领先优势，把里斯远远甩在了后面。这个决定使苏巴鲁—蒙哥马利车队的职业车手对兰斯非常反感，兰斯也知道这样做会使他失去在苏巴鲁—蒙哥马利车队的位置。另外，意大利车迷对美国人在比赛中领先感到愤怒，他们在路上扔玻璃和大头钉，希望兰斯的自行车爆胎。

[1] tacks　大头钉

但这一切都无济于事。兰斯以超过1分钟的领先优势第一个冲过终点线。这是在欧洲自行车赛事

was a rare American win in a European cycling event. The twenty-year-old amateur had finally made his mark[1] on the cycling world. That night, Carmichael told Lance something he would never forget. The coach said, "You're gonna win the Tour de France one day."

As Lance expected, Subaru-Montgomery kicked him off the team for disobeying orders. But Lance knew that if he kept winning races, he'd have his pick of teams.

Lance was building a reputation as a strong cyclist. He won the U.S. National Amateur Championship. He trained hard for the 1992 Olympics in Barcelona, Spain. He had looked forward to the 194-kilometer (120.5-mile) Olympic road race for years. At the time, only amateur cyclists were allowed to compete in the Olympics. Lance had remained an amateur just so he could race in the Olympics.

Lance gained strength as he approached the Olympics. He won three stages at a race in Spain. He won two more time trials back in the United States. And when the time came to qualify for the U.S. Olympic cycling team, he finished a solid second.

Chris Carmichael, who coached the Olympic team, tried to work out a winning strategy for Lance. He told one of Lance's teammates to make an early charge in the race. Carmichael hoped that all the other leading cyclists would go with the early charger. At the same time, Lance would stay behind and wait until the end to make an attack.

Early in the race, the plan seemed to be working perfectly. But when the time came for Lance to charge, he didn't have the energy. He pedaled as hard as he could, but he just couldn't catch up to the lead pack. He finished a disappointing fourteenth. Not only had he failed to win the gold medal (won by his friend Fabio Casartelli of Italy), he hadn't even been close to medaling.

[1] made his mark
出名

中美国人罕见的胜利。这位20岁的业余车手最终在自行车界出了名。那天晚上，卡米卡尔说的话令兰斯终生难忘，这位教练说："有一天你会成为环法自行车赛的冠军。"

正如兰斯所料，苏巴鲁—蒙哥马利车队因他不服从命令而将他踢出车队。但兰斯知道如果他继续赢得比赛，他就可以自己挑选车队。

兰斯逐渐以一位强壮的自行车选手而出名。他赢得了全美业余冠军赛的冠军。为了备战1992年在西班牙巴塞罗那举办的奥运会，他刻苦训练。他期待能参加奥运会的194公里（120.5英里）公路自行车赛已经好几年了。那时只有业余自行车选手才能参加奥运会，兰斯保持业余选手的身份就是为了能够参赛。

随着奥运会临近，兰斯不断取得进步：在西班牙的一次比赛中，他赢得了其中的3个赛段；在美国他赢得了两场计时赛的胜利；在美国奥运会自行车队选拔赛中，他以较大优势取得了第2名的成绩。

奥运会自行车队教练克里斯·卡米卡尔努力为兰斯制定了取得比赛胜利的策略。他让兰斯的一名队友在比赛开始阶段冲刺，希望其他领先的车手能够跟着这名较早冲刺的队友。同时兰斯呆在队伍后面，等待比赛最后发起进攻。

在比赛的开始阶段，这个计划似乎进展顺利，但轮到兰斯冲刺的时候，他却无力冲刺。他奋力踩着脚踏板，可还是赶不上前面的领先队伍。他取得了令人失望的第14名。他不仅没有夺得金牌（金牌被他的朋友——意大利车手法比奥·萨特利——夺得），而且和奖牌相距甚远。

With the Olympics past him, Lance knew it was time to finally turn professional. He was already making a living at cycling, but going pro[1] would allow him to collect prize money in international events. Coach Jim Ochowicz, nicknamed Och, signed Lance to ride for a cycling team sponsored by Motorola, a company that makes phones and other communications devices. Ochowicz was an old friend of Chris Carmichael, so he was already familiar with what Lance could do on a bike. "I want to go to Europe and be a pro," Lance told Ochowicz. "I don't want to just be good at it, I want to be the best."

With his new contract and new team, Lance packed his bags and moved to Italy. He and his teammates stayed in hotels during races. Eventually, Lance rented an apartment in Lake Como, Italy. The apartment served as his home base in Europe. He even learned to speak a little Spanish, Italian, French, and Dutch.

His first race as a pro was the 1992 Clásica San Sebastián[2] in northern Spain. This one-day race is one of ten in cycling's World Cup series. As the race got under way, Lance was battered[3] by cold winds and heavy rains, conditions he wasn't used to from his days in Texas. Soaking wet, Lance couldn't keep pace with the peloton. He wasn't the only one struggling, though. Several other riders simply quit the race. From the back of the pack, Lance thought about joining them. But quitting wasn't Lance's style. Instead, he fought through the pain and the cold and crossed the finish line. The crowd hooted[4] and made fun of Lance as he crossed, last of 111 finishers.

It was a terrible start to Lance's professional career. After a disappointing Olympics and an embarrassing first professional race, his confidence was as low as it had ever been. Lance thought about quitting the sport. Maybe it wasn't right for him. Maybe the competition at

奥运会结束后，兰斯知道该是最终转为职业自行车手的时候了。他靠自行车比赛已经能谋生，但转为职业选手后，他就可以在国际比赛中赢取奖金。摩托罗拉（美国一家制造电话和其他通信设备的公司）赞助的自行车队的教练吉姆·奥楚维茨（绰号奥楚）签下了兰斯。奥楚维茨是克里斯·卡米卡尔的老朋友，所以他很熟悉兰斯在自行车上的表现。兰斯告诉奥楚维茨："我要去欧洲比赛，我要做职业车手，我不想仅仅擅长这项运动，我想成为最优秀的。"

签了新合同、有了新车队后的兰斯整理行囊，移居意大利。他和队友在比赛期间住在宾馆里。最后，兰斯在意大利科摩湖租了一套公寓，作为他在欧洲的家。他甚至学会说一点西班牙语、意大利语、法语，还有荷兰语。

他作为职业选手参加的第一场比赛，是1992年在西班牙北部举行的圣塞巴斯蒂安精英赛。比赛为期一天，是自行车世界杯系列赛的10场比赛之一。比赛进行过程中，兰斯饱受冷风大雨之苦，当地的天气与得克萨斯的天气迥异，兰斯很不适应。浑身湿透的兰斯无法跟上主车群，但他并非唯一苦苦挣扎的选手。其他几个选手退出了比赛。落在后头的兰斯也想过和他们一样退出比赛，但是退出绝不是兰斯的行事风格。相反，他在伤痛和寒冷中拼搏，完成了比赛。当兰斯在111名完成比赛的选手中最后一个冲过终点线时，观众对他一边叫嚣一边取笑。

这对于兰斯的职业生涯是个糟糕的开端。经历了令人失望的奥运会比赛和令人难堪的首场职业比赛，他的信心前所未有的低落。兰斯想过退出这项运动，或许这并不适合他，或许职业比赛的竞

[1] pro <口> professional

[2] Clásica San Sebastián 圣塞巴斯蒂安精英赛（西班牙国内最大的自行车一日赛）

[3] battered （风、雨等）不断拍击

[4] hooted 轻蔑地大声喊叫

the professional level was just too tough. He called Chris Carmichael and told him about the disaster. His friend talked him out of quitting. Carmichael told Lance to learn from his failure and become a better cyclist because of it. Reluctantly, Lance agreed. He would keep trying.

Lance didn't have much time to feel sorry for himself. Two days later, he was riding in the Championship of Zurich in Switzerland. He had a lot at stake[1] in the race—his reputation, his pride, and, most important, his confidence in himself.

He started the race the best way he knew how—by attacking. He would leave strategy for another day. On this day, Lance was going all out[2]. He powered himself to the front of the peloton. As the race wore on, more and more cyclists fell back, unable to keep up with the blistering[3] pace. But not Lance. While he didn't win the race, his second-place finish proved that he belonged in the professional ranks. The finish was a much-needed boost[4] to the young cyclist's confidence.

Not long after his strong finish, Lance entered the Tour of the Mediterranean in Italy. He started the race out front and soon found himself riding alongside Italian cycling legend Moreno Argentin. When Argentin mistook Lance for another rider, the young American grew angry. He was insulted that the Italian didn't know his name. Lance taunted[5] and cursed at Argentin. He attacked and attacked until he ran out of energy. He'd ridden too hard.

The bad feelings between the two riders carried over into the next race, a one-day event in Italy called the Trophée Laigueglia. Again, Lance targeted Argentin. Again, he attacked. But since this was a shorter race, Lance didn't tire. As they sprinted toward the finish line, the four leaders pedaled with everything they had. With determination, Lance powered to the lead and crossed the finish line first. But behind him,

争过于严酷。他给克里斯·卡米卡尔打电话，告诉他自己的糟糕表现。作为朋友的克里斯说服了兰斯，使他放弃了退出自行车比赛的念头。卡米卡尔劝他总结失败的教训，从而成为更优秀的车手。兰斯勉强同意了，他会继续努力。

兰斯没有多少时间为自己感到难过，两天后他将参加瑞士苏黎世冠军赛。这次比赛，他处于成败关头，关系到很多东西——他的名声、自尊，还有最为重要的自信心。

他用他最熟悉的方式——冲刺——开始了比赛。他会把战术这码事留在另一天，这天他要全力以赴。他奋力前进，骑到了主车群的前面。随着比赛的进行，越来越多的选手跟不上，落在了后面。但兰斯没有。虽然兰斯没有赢得比赛，但他取得的第2名证明了他参加职业比赛的能力。这个名次对兰斯这个年轻车手的信心来说，起到了急需的鼓舞作用。

取得了这个优异的成绩后不久，兰斯参加了在意大利举行的环地中海自行车赛。比赛一开始他就冲到了前面，很快发现自己与意大利传奇车手莫雷诺·阿坚廷并肩骑行。阿坚廷把兰斯误认为另外一个选手，这个年轻的美国人便很生气。阿坚廷不知道自己的名字，这让他感觉受到了侮辱。兰斯对阿坚廷讥讽和咒骂。他不断地冲刺，直到用尽了所有力气。他骑得太猛了。

这两位车手之间的敌意被带入了下一场在意大利举行的名为莱归利亚杯经典赛的一日赛中。兰斯再次把矛头对准阿坚廷，而且再次发起冲刺。不过这次是短程赛，兰斯没有疲劳过度。在向终点冲刺时，领先的4个车手都使出了全身力气。充满决心的兰斯冲到了前面，第一个冲过了终点线。但在他的身后

[1] at stake 在危急之中

[2] going all out 全力以赴

[3] blistering 极快的

[4] boost 激励；促进

[5] taunted 斥责；嘲笑；讥讽

something unusual happened. Argentin slammed[1] on his brakes. He let the other two riders cross the finish line before him.

At first, this action confused Lance. But quickly, he understood the veteran[2] cyclist's message. Argentin had finished fourth on purpose. The top three finishers stand together on the podium[3] to receive medals. Argentin preferred finishing fourth to standing next to Lance. It was the biggest insult he could give the young American. It was also a lesson that Lance took to heart. He realized that he needed to stop making enemies.

As summer approached, Lance was getting more attention, both for his success and for his racing style. Many cyclists enjoy the attention that success brings. But Lance wasn't ready for it. "I don't want to be the big star," he said. "I don't want to be bothered. I want to be left alone really and allowed to race."

[1] slammed 猛击

[2] veteran 经验丰富的; 老练的

[3] podium 讲台; 指挥台

发生了不寻常的事情：阿坚廷猛地刹车，让其他两个选手在他之前冲过了终点线。

起初兰斯对此迷惑不解，但很快他就明白了这个自行车老将的用意。阿坚廷是故意取得第4名的。前3名一起站在领奖台上领奖，阿坚廷宁愿得第4，也不愿意和兰斯站在一起。这是阿坚廷能给兰斯这个年轻美国人的最大的羞辱。这也是兰斯铭记于心的一个教训，他意识到他得停止树敌了。

随着夏季的来临，因为兰斯取得的成绩和他的比赛风格，他受到了越来越多的关注。很多车手很享受伴随成功而来的人们的关注，但兰斯对此还没有做好准备。他说："我不想当个大明星，我不想被打搅。我想真正不受干扰地参加比赛。"

CHAPTER FOUR

RISING STAR

崭露头角

The summer of 1993 was a big time in Lance's career. The exciting news in the American cycling world was a $1 million bonus being offered to any rider who could win the Triple Crown of Cycling, which was composed of three of the biggest races in the United States. The Thrift drug company offered the bonus as a way to get publicity.

Because the three races are very different, it seemed unlikely that one rider could win them all. He would have to be an expert sprinter, stage racer, and climber. The executives at Thrift never expected to have to pay the bonus.

Lance disagreed. He was making a good salary. But $1 million was a whole lot of money. It would make life comfortable for him and his mother, who had worked so hard to help him succeed.

The chase for the Triple Crown began in Pittsburgh, Pennsylvania, with the Thrift Drug Classic, a one-day sprint. Lance won the event. Next, he went to West Virginia for the West Virginia Mountain Classic. There, his powerful climbing drove him to victory in the six-day stage race. He was two-thirds of the way to his goal. All that remained was the U.S. Pro Championships in Philadelphia, Pennsylvania.

Lance was one of 120 riders who lined up to start the grueling, 156-mile lap race. The media was everywhere. In a nation where cycling isn't a big sport, Lance's quest for the Triple Crown had captured the public's attention. An estimated five hundred thousand people lined the streets of Philadelphia to watch the race.

Early on, Lance hung back, determined to ride a smart race. He wouldn't attack too soon and wear himself out. He rode along with the pack for the first 130 miles. Then, as

1993年的夏天是兰斯在职业生涯中大获成功的时刻。美国自行车界有一条激动人心的消息：谁能赢得由美国3个重大自行车赛事组成的自行车三冠赛，就能获得100万美元的奖金。“平价”医药公司提供了这笔奖金，以此来宣传自己。

因为这3个赛事彼此迥异，因此任何一名车手都似乎很难赢得这3个比赛的冠军。谁若想成功，就必须同时是冲刺专家、赛段比赛高手和爬坡名将。“平价”的管理者根本没准备支付这笔奖金。

兰斯不这么看。虽然他的收入不错，但100万美元毕竟是一大笔钱。有了它，兰斯和努力工作帮助自己成功的妈妈就能过得很舒服。

兰斯参加了在宾夕法尼亚州的匹兹堡举行的为期一天的短距离比赛——“平价”经典赛，开始了三冠赛的征途。兰斯赢得了比赛胜利。接下来，他参加了在西弗吉尼亚举行的西弗吉尼亚山地经典赛。他强劲的爬坡能力帮助他赢得了这个为期6天的赛段比赛的冠军。他离他的目标只剩下三分之一的路程。剩下的就是在宾夕法尼亚州的费城举行的美国职业冠军赛。

这个残酷的绕圈赛长达156英里，共有120名选手参赛。比赛现场到处都是新闻媒体。在美国，自行车运动不是一项广受关注的体育项目，但兰斯对三冠赛的追逐吸引了公众的目光。据估计，费城大街上夹道观看者有50万人。

比赛开始，决心智取比赛的兰斯骑在了后面。他不想过早发起冲刺而耗尽体力。在比赛的前130英里，他骑在主车群里。当

the peloton approached one of the steepest climbs of the course, Lance decided it was time to go. He later described himself as being in a rage. He screamed as he pedaled, blowing past his competition and opening up a huge lead.

As he crossed the finish line, reporters rushed to speak to him. Lance hadn't just won the Triple Crown. He'd also won the U.S. Pro Championships by the largest margin in the history of the race. The crowd roared as Lance gave his mom a big hug. Later, as he stood on the podium to accept his trophy, Lance broke down in tears of joy.

Lance was looking forward to entering the 1993 Tour de France. The race, which winds throughout France and sometimes into neighboring countries, is the most famous and most grueling cycling race of them all. But first, Lance prepared for the Tour DuPont, a miniature[1] American version of the Tour de France. Lance was hot and entered the race as one of the cyclists to beat. Right away, he proved that he would be a force, finishing second in the opening time trial.

Throughout the race, Lance battled Mexico's Raul Alcala for the lead. They raced through Delaware, Virginia, and North Carolina. They climbed the slopes of the Appalachian Mountains[2], side by side. Neither man could build much of a lead on the other. Finally, entering the last stage, Lance trailed Alcala by 19 seconds.

Lance had 36.5 miles to make up that 19 seconds. The final stage was a time trial, so the riders wouldn't start alongside one another. Since Alcala was the race leader, he started last. Lance started a few minutes before him.

Lance knew he was in trouble when Alcala began to catch him. When the Mexican cyclist passed him, all hope of winning seemed lost. Then Alcala's bike had a flat tire.

队伍到达最陡的爬坡路段之一时，兰斯决定是时候冲刺了。事后他形容自己“勃然大怒”，一边骑车一边大叫着超过其他选手，取得了很大的领先优势。

兰斯冲过终点线后，记者们冲上前去采访他。兰斯不仅赢得了三冠赛的胜利，而且以美国职业冠军赛历史上最大的领先优势赢得了比赛。兰斯热烈拥抱他妈妈时，围观人群一片欢呼。随后，当他站在领奖台上接受奖杯时，他哭了起来，流下了喜悦的泪水。

兰斯期待着参加1993年的环法自行车赛。环法比赛是自行车比赛中最著名也是最令人筋疲力尽的赛事，它的路线环绕法国，有时也会进入邻国境内。但首先兰斯备战的是杜邦大奖赛，这是环法比赛的小型美国翻版。兰斯作为夺冠的热门选手参加了比赛。很快他证明了自己的实力，在比赛开始的计时赛中取得亚军。

整个比赛，兰斯都在和墨西哥选手劳尔·阿卡拉争夺领先的位置。他们一路竞争着穿过特拉华州、弗吉尼亚州和北卡罗来纳州，他们肩并肩爬过阿巴拉契亚山脉的陡坡，谁都不能占据很大的领先优势。最终进入最后一个赛段时，兰斯落后阿卡拉19秒。

兰斯得在36.5英里的距离内弥补那19秒的差距。最后一个赛段是个计时赛，所以车手们出发的时间各不相同。阿卡拉是比赛的领先者，所以最后一个出发。兰斯比他早几分钟出发。

当阿卡拉开始要追上自己的时候，兰斯知道自己处境不妙。当这位墨西哥车手超过自己的时候，兰斯似乎失去了赢得比赛的全部希望。这时阿卡拉的自行车有一个轮胎爆了。兰斯超过

[1] miniature 微型的；小规模的

[2] the Appalachian Mountains 阿巴拉契亚山脉（北美洲东部的山脉）

Lance sailed past the leader, hopeful that he could earn back all the time he had lost. But Alcala's team quickly helped him change the tire and got him back on the course. The Mexican crossed the finish line with a 46-second lead.

Next up for Lance was the Tour de France. Despite his success in the United States, nobody expected him to be a factor in the race. At twenty-one, he was young and still a newcomer. And he was an American competing in an event dominated by more-experienced Europeans.

Lance wanted to make his mark. He targeted the race's eighth stage, a 184-kilometer (114-mile) ride from Châlons-sur-Marne to Verdun, France. He wasn't ready to win the whole race, but Lance could win a single stage, still a huge accomplishment. He started off the stage riding and drafting with the peloton. With about 10 kilometers (6 miles) to go, Lance and a small group of riders broke away from the pack. The sprint was on.

As the finish line approached, Lance made a move to pass to the right, but Irish cyclist Stephen Roche moved over to block him. With only 100 meters (330 feet) to go, Lance let out a scream so loud that it surprised Roche, breaking his concentration for a moment. That break was all the young American needed. He powered past the leader, almost running into a roadside barrier as he did, and crossed the finish line first. Lance had achieved his goal by winning a stage at the Tour de France—becoming one of the youngest riders ever to do so.

As high as Lance was from his win, the good feelings didn't last long. Only four stages later, he dropped out of the race. After a cold, brutal climb through the Alps, he knew he could go no farther. He told reporters that the mountains were just "too long and too cold."

了他，希望能弥补自己和他之间的差距。但阿卡拉的团队很快给他更换了轮胎，帮他重回赛道。这位墨西哥车手以46秒的领先优势冲过了终点线。

接下来兰斯就要面对环法比赛了。尽管他在美国取得了成功，但在这次比赛中没人看好他。这个21岁的年轻人还属于新人。他是美国人，而他参加的这次比赛由经验更为丰富的欧洲选手所主导。

兰斯想出名。他瞄准了比赛的第8赛段——从法国马恩河畔沙隆到凡尔登。兰斯还未准备好赢得整个比赛，但他能赢下一个赛段，那也算很大的成就了。这个赛段的比赛一开始，兰斯骑行在主车群的后面。当比赛还剩下10公里（6英里）时，兰斯和一小群车手从车群中冲了出来。冲刺开始了。

快接近终点线时，兰斯突然骑到了右边，但爱尔兰车手斯蒂芬·罗齐挡在了他的前面。比赛还剩下100米（330英尺），兰斯突然大叫一声，声音非常响，罗齐对此很诧异，暂时分散了自己的注意力。这个空当正是这位年轻的美国车手所需要的。他发力骑过前面的领先者，差点撞到了路边的障碍，第一个冲过了终点线。兰斯实现了在环法比赛中赢下一个赛段的目标——也成为完成这个目标的最年轻的车手之一。

取得胜利的兰斯情绪高涨，但这份好心情并没有持续很长时间。4个赛段之后，他就退出了比赛。在寒冷的天气里完成了在阿尔卑斯山的一个残酷的爬坡赛段之后，他知道他不能再前进了。他告诉记者，山区的路程“太长了，（天气）太冷了”。

Lance's problems continued in his very next race, the Championship of Zurich. It was a typical failure—he attacked too soon and didn't have anything left at the finish. He vowed[1] not to do the same thing a week later at the World Championships in Oslo[2], Norway. The Tour de France may be cycling's most famous race, but the Worlds are almost as important to many riders. The title of world champion is one that every cyclist wants.

The race, 257 kilometers (160 miles) over fourteen laps, looked like it would be a problem for Lance. A heavy rain fell, drenching[3] the competitors and making the course slippery. The conditions reminded Lance of his failure in his first professional race in Spain. But this time, the young American overcame the obstacle. He stayed in the front of the peloton throughout the first thirteen laps. He crashed twice, as did many of the riders, but was not hurt. After one crash, he fell far behind the peloton. But his teammates dropped back and joined him, helping him draft back to the lead pack.

On the final lap, as the riders approached the second-to-last climb, Lance knew it was time to attack. The leaders, including the Tour de France champion, Miguel Indurain, looked tired. They didn't seem ready for a strong push to the finish. But Lance was ready. He charged, and by the top of the climb, he had the tiniest of leads. He sped down the hill and pedaled hard into the final climb. He held his lead as he approached the final descent.

As he went down the hill at top speed, Lance knew the danger. At any moment, the bike's tires could lose their grip[4]. He was risking a huge crash. But he didn't pull back at all. He was willing to risk it for the chance at the championship. "When I went, I knew I had to go with everything I had," he said. "It was all or nothing at that

[1] vowed 发誓
[2] Oslo 奥斯陆（挪威首都）
[3] drenching 使浸透；淋透
[4] grip 控制

在接下来的一场比赛——苏黎世冠军赛——中，兰斯的问题依然存在。这是一场典型的失败——他过早开始冲刺，快到终点时却没有了力气。一周后在挪威奥斯陆将举行世界冠军赛，他发誓那时将不再犯同样的错误。环法比赛是自行车界最著名的比赛，但对很多车手而言，世界冠军赛同样重要。每个车手都渴望世界冠军的头衔。

比赛的路程长达257公里（160英里），共进行14圈，看起来对兰斯而言将很艰苦。下了一场大雨，选手们都湿透了，路段也变得很滑。这种情况使兰斯想起了自己在西班牙的首场职业比赛的失败。但这次，这个年轻的美国人克服了困难，在前13圈里都保持在主车群的前面。很多选手都摔倒过，兰斯也一样，他摔了两次，但没有受伤。有次他摔倒后，远远落在了主车群后面。但他的队友减慢速度和他一起前进，并在前面为他减小空气阻力，帮他回到了处于领先的车群中。

当选手们接近最后一圈中倒数第2个爬坡路段时，兰斯知道冲刺的时刻到了。领先的选手们，包括环法比赛冠军米盖尔·安杜兰，看起来都很疲惫，似乎无法用冲刺来完成比赛。但兰斯准备好了。他冲刺起来，在爬坡路段的最高处取得了微弱的领先优势。他冲下山坡，快速蹬着脚踏板，向最后一个爬坡路段冲刺。快接近最后一个爬坡路段时，他依然保持着领先。

当兰斯全速冲下山坡时，他知道其中的危险。自行车的轮胎在任何时候都可能会失去控制，他在冒着发生严重碰撞的危险。但他丝毫没有退却。为了赢得冠军赛的机会，他甘愿冒险。他说：“当我冲下来时，我知道我必须全力以赴了。在那一刻，胜

point—if I'd been caught, I wouldn't have had anything left for a sprint."

At one point, Lance looked over his shoulder to see how big his lead was. When he didn't see any other riders, he felt a moment of panic. Had he miscounted[1] his laps? Had he attacked too soon, with another whole lap to go? If so, he would be doomed. But no, he hadn't miscounted. It was the final lap, and he was all alone. What Lance didn't know at the time was that his teammates had helped him again. They had ridden together to the front of the peloton and then slowed down, slowing down everyone else as well.

As he crossed the finish line, Lance started celebrating. He pumped his fists and jumped off the bike to hug his mother. He was the world champion, and there wasn't anyone else he wanted to celebrate with.

After the race, Lance heard that Norway's King Harald wanted to meet and congratulate the race winner. Lance and Linda went together to see the king. But when they approached the guard outside the king's room, their escort said that only Lance could enter. His mother would have to wait elsewhere.

Linda had sat outside in the pouring rain for the entire race. She had been a huge source of support for her son, and Lance wasn't about to leave her behind. He took Linda by the arm and turned around. If they weren't going in together, he wasn't going in at all. As they walked away, the escort shouted after them. Linda could come too. Smiling, they entered to meet King Harald.

Lance had made one of the highest achievements in cycling. But still, he thought about the Tour de France. That was how a cyclist really made his mark. The world's most famous cyclists had one thing in common—they were Tour champions. Lance wanted his name listed alongside Greg LeMond, Miguel Indurain, and Eddy Merckx.

[1] miscounted 算错；数错

败在此一举——如果我摔倒了，就没有任何可能再次冲刺了。”

有那么一刻，兰斯扭头去看自己的领先优势有多大。当他看不到其他任何选手时，他感到一阵恐惧。他数错圈数了？他过早冲刺，离比赛结束还有整整一圈？如果是这样，他就输定了。但是他并没有数错。这是最后一圈，而就他一个人骑在前面。在那个时候兰斯所不知道的是，他的队友再次帮助了他。他们一起骑在主车群的前面，然后慢下来，这样其他选手都得慢下来。

当兰斯冲过了终点线时，他开始庆祝胜利。他挥舞着拳头，跳下自行车去拥抱母亲。他是世界冠军了，他不想和其他任何人庆祝胜利。

比赛结束后，兰斯听说挪威国王哈罗德想接见并祝贺比赛胜利者。兰斯和琳达一起去见国王，但当他们走近国王房间外的护卫时，他们的随同人员说只有兰斯能进去，他母亲必须在其他地方等着。

整个比赛，琳达冒着瓢泼大雨，坐在外面。一直以来，她为儿子提供了强有力的支持，所以兰斯不打算把她留在后头。他抓起琳达的手，转身离去。如果他们不能一起进去，那他也不进去。他们要走开时，随同人员在他们身后喊道，琳达也可以进去。他们微笑着进去见国王哈罗德。

兰斯已经取得自行车界最重要的成就之一。但他依然想着环法比赛。环法比赛才是一个自行车手真正扬名立万的途径。世界最著名的自行车手都有一个共同点——他们都是环法比赛的冠军。兰斯渴望自己的名字和格雷格·勒芒、米盖尔·安杜兰和埃迪·墨克斯并列在一起。

But there was a problem. Lance wasn't a strong stage racer. He had done well in the Tour DuPont, but that race was nothing compared to the long, painful ordeal[1] of the Tour de France. Some people didn't think Lance had the body to last the whole race. He was a big, muscular rider at 5 feet, 10 inches and 175 pounds. That build[2] worked great for sprints. But in the Tour's long mountain stages, all the extra weight just slowed a rider down.

Lance had his doubts too, but he also had his dreams. He started training differently. He tried to slim[3] down. He worked on his endurance. If he was going to take the next step in cycling, he needed to work hard. He was willing to do whatever it took to become a great stage racer.

The year 1994 was a time of transition[4] for Lance. He kept improving. A second-place finish at the Clásica San Sebastián was a big moment for him — he hadn't forgotten his embarrassing last-place finish there in his first professional race. He also had some success at the Tour DuPont, winning one stage and finishing second overall to Russia's Viatcheslav Ekimov. But victories were hard to come by[5]. Lance's backers[6] and teammates sometimes grew impatient with his lack of results.

But Lance had a plan. In 1995 he targeted the Tour DuPont as a race he wanted to win. He'd finished second there twice. A win would help establish him as a real stage racer.

Lance struggled during the early stages of the race. But as the race moved into the mountains, he took control. He dominated the stage 4 climb and moved into first place by more than 2 minutes. He widened his lead the next day, winning the stage 5 time trial. This time, Lance never looked back. He won stage 9 and then cruised to a 2-minute victory over Ekimov. Once again, Lance's career was on the rise.

但有一个问题，那就是兰斯不是一个优秀的赛段比赛选手。他在杜邦大奖赛中表现优异，但和艰苦漫长的环法比赛相比，杜邦赛不值一提。有人认为兰斯不具备完成整个比赛的身体素质。他身高5英尺10英寸，体重175磅，高大强健，这样的体格非常适合短距离比赛。但在环法比赛中的山地赛段，多余的体重只会使车手慢下来。

兰斯也怀疑过自己，但他同样怀有梦想。他改变了训练方法，努力瘦身，刻苦训练耐力。如果他想在自行车界取得进一步的成绩，他得刻苦训练。为了能成为一名伟大的赛段比赛车手，做什么他都愿意。

1994年对兰斯来说是转变的一年。他不断在进步。在圣塞巴斯蒂安精英赛中夺得第2名对他而言意义重大——他没有忘记他在这里的首场职业比赛中取得的最后一名给他带来的尴尬。他在杜邦大奖赛中也取得了成功，赢下一个赛段，总成绩第2，仅次于俄罗斯车手维阿切斯拉夫·爱基莫夫。但胜利非常难得，兰斯的赞助商和队友有时候变得没有耐心，因为兰斯缺乏好成绩。

但兰斯有自己的计划。1995年，他把夺冠的目标锁定为杜邦大奖赛。他在这里已经取得了两次第2名，一场胜利可以确立他作为一名真正的赛段比赛车手的地位。

在比赛开始阶段，兰斯有些吃力，但当比赛进入山地赛段后，他取得了对比赛的控制。他主宰了第4赛段的坡路，以超过2分钟的优势获得了领先。第2天赢下第5赛段的计时赛后，他扩大了领先优势。这一次，兰斯从未回头看。他又赢下第9赛段，然后以比爱基莫夫领先2分钟的优势赢得了比赛。兰斯的职业生涯又一次处于上升期。

[1] ordeal 严峻的考验；折磨

[2] build 体格；体型

[3] slim （用运动、节食等）减轻体重；变苗条

[4] transition 转变，转换

[5] come by （常指意外地或偶然地）得到，获得

[6] backers 帮助者（尤指资助者）

CHAPTER **FIVE**

LIFE AND DEATH

生死之间

5. Life and Death

Lance went to France in the summer of 1995 feeling good. Everything seemed to be going his way. He and his Motorola teammates were excited about the Tour de France, and this time, Lance intended to finish.

Fourteen days into the race, Lance was still riding strong. He knew he wasn't going to win the race, but that wasn't his goal. He just wanted to prove he could finish.

But everything changed on July 18, the day of stage 15. Lance was riding through a mountain pass[1], one of the steepest downhill sections of the race. In a descent[2] like this one, riders go single file[3] down the slope at speeds of more than 60 miles per hour. If one rider crashes, it can set up a bad chain reaction[4]. That's what happened to a group ahead of Lance that day.

As Lance rode by, he saw there had been a crash. A large group of people was gathered around someone lying on the ground. Lance was speeding by, and he didn't know that the person was his teammate Fabio Casartelli. Casartelli, from Italy, had been one of about twenty riders involved in the crash. He had slammed his head into a concrete curb. Tour officials called for a helicopter to fly the injured cyclist to a hospital. But it was too late. Casartelli died in the helicopter.

A few minutes later, Lance learned what had happened to his friend and teammate. He was crushed and felt ill. But he had to finish the stage.

That night, Lance and the rest of the Motorola team had to decide what to do. Would they keep riding or quit the race? Lance wanted to stop racing. Suddenly, the Tour didn't seem important anymore. He didn't know if he had

1995年夏天，感觉良好的兰斯来到法国。一切似乎都很顺利。他和他所在的摩托罗拉车队的队友对即将到来的环法比赛都很兴奋。这一次，兰斯想完成比赛。

离比赛还有14天时，兰斯的骑行状态仍然不错。他知道他赢不了比赛，但冠军不是他的目标。他只想证明自己能够完成比赛。

但在7月18日的第15赛段的比赛日中，一切都改变了。当时兰斯正骑过一个山口，这也是比赛中最陡的下坡路段之一。在这样的下坡路段，选手们以每小时60多英里的速度呈一字形前进。如果一个选手摔倒，就会引起可怕的连锁反应。那一天，兰斯前面的车队就发生了这样的连锁反应。

兰斯骑车经过时，看到发生了碰撞事故。一个人躺在地上，一群人围着他。兰斯快速骑过，他并不知道躺着的那人就是自己的队友——意大利车手法比奥·萨特利，他是发生连环撞车的约20人中的一个。他的头部撞上了水泥护栏。赛事官员呼叫了一架直升机把伤者送往医院，但是太迟了，萨特利死在了直升机里。

几分钟后，兰斯得知了发生在他的朋友兼队友身上的事情。他崩溃了，感到十分难过。但他必须完成比赛。

那天晚上，兰斯和摩托罗拉车队的队友必须决定该怎么办。是该坚持比赛还是退出比赛呢？兰斯想退出。突然之间，环法比赛不再重要。他不清楚自己是否还有意志或愿望继续骑

[1] pass　山口，要隘

[2] descent　下坡路；下降

[3] file　纵列

[4] chain reaction　连锁反应

the will or desire to get back on his bike. But Fabio's wife talked to the team. She told them that her husband would want them to finish. So that's what they did.

The next day, for stage 16, the entire peloton rode together. No one tried to win. It was their way of honoring their lost friend. The racing could wait a day.

Stage 18 into the city of Limoges took on a new importance to Lance. Casartelli had been looking forward to that stage. He had hoped it would be his stage to win. Since his friend couldn't win it anymore, Lance decided to take Casartelli's place.

Halfway through the stage, Lance was riding with a group of about twenty-five cyclists. The race leader, Miguel Indurain, was heading the pack. The group slowly pulled away from the other riders. With about 40 kilometers (25 miles) to go, they hit a small descent. Lance didn't want to wait any longer. He charged. His attack came as a complete surprise to the other leaders. It was too early in the stage for a sprint to the finish. And a downhill attack was almost unheard of—it was dangerous and considered by most to be poor strategy. Lance's move didn't make any sense, and the other riders weren't sure what to do.

Lance took advantage of the confusion. In no time, he had a 30-second lead. The lead grew and grew. He finally crossed the finish line a full minute ahead of everyone else. As he crossed, he raised both arms, looked up, and pointed into the sky to honor his lost friend. He continued his tribute[1] to Casartelli by completing the Tour, finishing in thirty-sixth place overall.

The tragedy at the 1995 Tour was hard on Lance, but other than that, his career was going great. The year 1996 started out as Lance's best year yet. The cycling world saw him as one of the sport's biggest stars. He won an

上他的自行车。但法比奥的妻子和车队谈话，她告诉他们她的丈夫希望他们完成比赛。于是他们决定继续比赛。

在第2天第16赛段的比赛中，整个主车群一起前进，没有人试图取胜。这是他们纪念失去的朋友的方式。竞争可以等到明天再进行。

进入利摩日市的第18赛段对兰斯而言有了新的重要意义。萨特利一直期待着这个赛段，希望自己能够赢下它。既然自己的朋友不可能再赢得这个赛段，兰斯决定替他获胜。

比赛过半时，兰斯和一个约有25名选手组成的车群一起骑行。赛事领先者米盖尔·安杜兰骑在车群前面。这组选手慢慢与其他选手拉开了距离。离赛段终点还有40公里（25英里）时，他们到达一小段下坡路。兰斯不想再等了，他发起冲刺。其他选手都对他的冲刺感到非常奇怪：赛段进行到这里就冲刺还太早，而且在下坡路冲刺几乎闻所未闻——这很危险，而且大多数人认为这是拙劣的战术。兰斯的举动并不合理，其他选手都不知道如何是好。

兰斯利用这个混乱，很快取得了30秒的领先。领先优势越来越大，最后他以整整1分钟的领先优势冲过终点线。当他撞线时，他举起双臂，抬起头，把手指向天空，向他失去的朋友致敬。对萨特利的致敬一直持续到比赛结束，他最终以总排名第36位的成绩完成了比赛。

1995年环法比赛中的悲剧使兰斯难以承受，但除此之外，他的事业进展顺利。1996年是兰斯开局最好的一年：自行车界把他看做该项运动最大的明星之一。春天，他在比利时赢得了一场重

[1] tribute 称赞，颂辞

important race in Belgium in the spring and then won the Tour DuPont again that summer.

Lance looked forward to the Tour de France, where he was finally considered a contender[1] for the victory. He also hoped to win at the Olympics in Atlanta, Georgia. (By then, professionals were allowed to compete in the Olympic Games.) Lance didn't always feel his best, but he was training hard and still finishing well, so he didn't worry too much.

As the Tour de France got under way, things started to go wrong. Early in the race, heavy rains poured down on the cyclists. Lance pedaled on, but the effort took its toll[2] on him. Soon he was coughing. His throat was sore. His back hurt. He couldn't keep going. Since the Olympics started just a few days after the Tour ended, Lance knew what he had to do. He dropped out of[3] the Tour and tried to get himself healthy for the road race in Atlanta.

But that didn't work out, either. Lance still felt weak during the Olympics. He finished sixth in the time trial and struggled to twelfth in the road race. His body just couldn't give him what he needed. His muscles ached, and he was always sleepy.

A few bad finishes didn't slow down the demand for Lance Armstrong, though. He signed a contract worth $2.5 million to join a French racing team called Cofidis. At home in Texas, he moved into a mansion on the banks of Lake Austin. He had a boat, a sports car, and a swimming pool.

A few days after his twenty-fifth birthday that September, Lance and his friends were celebrating. But Lance had to leave the party early with a terrible headache. The headache got worse and worse, and there was nothing he could do to make it go away. "It was the kind of headache you see in the movies, a knee-buckling,

要比赛的胜利，随后在夏天又再次赢下杜邦大奖赛。

兰斯期待着环法比赛，在那里他最终被视为冠军的有力争夺者。他还希望能赢下在佐治亚州亚特兰大举行的奥运会比赛（那时候职业选手已被允许参加奥运会）。兰斯并不总是感觉最好，但他刻苦训练，训练完成得也不错，所以他也不太担心。

当环法比赛开始进行时，问题开始出现了。比赛一开始，大雨倾盆，雨水倾泻在选手们身上。兰斯继续蹬踏板，但他的努力对他的身体造成了损害。很快他开始咳嗽，喉咙和背部也开始疼痛。他不能继续前进。环法比赛结束后几天，奥运会就将开始，所以兰斯清楚自己该做什么。他退出了环法比赛，努力使自己康复，以便迎接在亚特兰大举行的公路赛。

但这种做法并没有奏效。在奥运会比赛中，兰斯依然感到很虚弱，在计时赛中他取得第6名，在公路赛中他吃力地完成比赛，取得了第12名。他力不从心，肌肉很痛，也总是想睡觉。

但几场比赛失利并没有降低兰斯·阿姆斯特朗受欢迎的程度。他签了一份价值250万美元的合同，加入了一支名为科菲蒂斯的法国车队。在老家得克萨斯，他搬进了奥斯丁湖畔的一所大房子里，他拥有一艘船、一辆跑车和一个游泳池。

那年9月，他的25岁生日后没几天，兰斯和朋友们正在搞庆祝活动，但兰斯因为一阵剧烈的头痛不得不提前离开聚会。头痛越来越剧烈，他无论怎么做都无法消除。他后来在他的《这与自行车无关》一书中写道：“那就是你在

[1] contender 竞争者

[2] took its toll 造成损失（或危害、伤亡等）

[3] dropped out of 退出

head-between-your-hands, brain-crusher," Lance later wrote in his book *It's Not About the Bike*.

The headache wasn't his only problem. A few days later, he was coughing up blood. Then one of his testicles[1] began to swell[2] and hurt. He tried to ignore all these problems. He tried to keep training and pretend nothing was wrong. But he couldn't do it. Something *was* wrong. His doctor sent him to a specialist, Dr. Jim Reeves. Reeves wanted to run some tests to find out what was happening.

Lance lay on a table for more than an hour for a test called an ultrasound[3]. When the test was done, the doctor told him he needed another test—a chest X-ray. That didn't make any sense to Lance. Why did they want to look at his chest? He was getting upset, but he did as hc was told.

Lance returned to Reeves's office. It was getting late, and Lance knew the doctor normally would have gone home by then. That worried him.

Reeves looked at the X-rays, then looked at Lance. "This is a serious situation," he said. "It looks like testicular cancer."

Lance was shocked. *Cancer*. This wasn't just a danger to his career. It was a danger to his life.

Reeves explained more. He told Lance that the cancer had spread from his testicle to his lungs. It was possible to cure the cancer, but time was precious. The faster treatment started, the better Lance's chances would be. First of all, Lance needed surgery immediately to remove his testicle.

Lance went home in a daze[4]. He had to tell his friends and his mother. It was a tough night. But his friends supported him. They told him everything would be all right.

电影中看到的令人双手抱头、跪在地上、头痛欲裂的那种头痛。”

头痛并不是他唯一的问题：几天后他开始咳血，然后一个睾丸开始肿大疼痛。他试图忽略所有这些问题，努力保持训练，想假装没有发生任何问题。但他做不到。真的出问题了。他的医生让他去见一个专家——吉姆·里维斯医生。里维斯医生打算进行一些检查来看看到底发生了什么问题。

兰斯在一张桌子上躺了一个多小时，接受名为超声波的检查。当检查结束后，医生告诉他，他得再做一个检查——胸透。兰斯不理解，为什么他们想检查他的胸部？他开始感到不安，但他还是照做了。

兰斯返回里维斯的办公室时，天渐渐黑了。兰斯有些担心，因为他知道，通常这个时候，医生都已经回家了。

里维斯看了看X光片，然后看着兰斯，说：“情况很严重，看起来像睾丸癌。”

兰斯非常震惊：癌症。这样的话，不光是他的职业生涯，更重要的是，他的生命都将面临危险。

里维斯进行了详细的解释，他告诉兰斯，癌症已经从他的睾丸扩散到了肺部，癌症有可能被治愈，但时间宝贵。治疗开始越早，兰斯康复的机会越大。首先，兰斯需要立即做手术切除睾丸。

兰斯精神恍惚地回到家。他得告诉他的朋友和妈妈。那个夜晚很难熬，但他的朋友很支持他，告诉他一切都会好的。

[1] testicles 睾丸

[2] swell 肿大；膨胀

[3] ultrasound 超声波

[4] in a daze 晕迷状

Early the next morning, Lance returned to the hospital for surgery. His friends filled the waiting room during the three-hour procedure. Finally, the good news came. The surgery had been a success. Lance was in a great deal of pain, but he was hopeful that the worst was behind him.

That hope quickly faded[1], though. More tests revealed that the cancer had spread more than previously thought. It was a stage-three cancer, meaning it had advanced a long way and would be harder to treat. For the next three months, Lance would need powerful chemotherapy[2] (chemo), a kind of cancer treatment that can be very hard on the patient. The drugs used in the treatment kill cancer cells, but they also kill many healthy cells. Patients often lose a lot of weight. Their hair may fall out[3]. It is a very unpleasant way to live. But without treatment, Lance would die. With the treatment, his chances of living were better than 60 percent.

Lance didn't let the treatments get him down. He tried to stay positive. His body handled the drugs without too many side effects[4]. Once he was healed from the surgery, he even rode his bike a little every night.

Lance talked to new doctors about his treatments. He wanted the doctors to use drugs that wouldn't destroy his muscles or hurt his chances of returning to cycling someday. But as his doctors worked, they didn't like the test results they got back. Something was still wrong. Lance's cancer wasn't going away. More bad news was on the way—the cancer had spread to Lance's brain. He had two tumors[5] there.

When she found out, Linda broke down in tears. She knew what this news meant. Lance's chances of survival had just dropped—by a lot. Lance's doctors didn't say so at the time, but when they found the brain tumors, they thought his hopes of recovery were almost gone. The doctors told Lance that his chances for survival were about 50 percent. But that wasn't what they really

第2天一早，兰斯返回医院接受手术。在手术进行的3个小时里，他的朋友挤满了等候室。最终传来了好消息：手术成功了。兰斯忍受着巨大的疼痛，但他充满希望，相信最坏的情况已经过去。

但希望很快消失。更多的检查显示，癌症扩散的情况比预先想的要严重。这是第3级癌症，也就是说，病情发展到了更严重的地步，并且更难治愈。接下来的3个月里，兰斯需要强力的化学治疗。化疗是一种治疗癌症的疗法，病人可能会非常痛苦。化疗使用的药物能杀死癌症细胞，但也会杀死很多健康细胞。病人通常会减轻很多体重，他们的头发会脱落。化疗是一种令病人很痛苦的生存方法。但兰斯不做化疗就会死，做了化疗，他的生存几率超过60%。

兰斯没有让治疗打垮自己。他努力保持积极乐观。他的身体用药后没有出现过多的副作用。在手术伤口刚刚愈合后，他甚至每晚都骑一会儿自行车。

兰斯和他的新医生谈论他的治疗情况，他想让医生使用不伤害肌肉的药物，这样他有一天重回自行车赛场的希望就不会破灭。但是在治疗过程中，医生对他们得到的检查结果忧心忡忡。问题依然存在，兰斯的癌症并没有消失。更多的坏消息接踵而至——癌症已经扩散到兰斯的大脑，他脑部有两个肿瘤。

当琳达得知这个消息后失声痛哭。她知道这个消息意味着什么：兰斯活下来的几率降低了——降低了很多。兰斯的医生起初不这么说，但当他们发现了脑部肿瘤后，他们认为他康复的希望几乎不存在了。医生告诉兰斯，他活下来的几率是50%，但这并不是他

[1] faded 消失；褪色

[2] chemotherapy 化学治疗

[3] fall out （头发、牙齿等）脱落

[4] side effects 副作用

[5] tumors 肿瘤

thought. Privately, the doctors didn't expect him to live.

The next step for Lance was brain surgery. The idea was terrifying. The surgery could damage his vision and his coordination[1]. If things went wrong, he would never ride again. But he had no choice. The tumors had to come out. He just had to hope for the best. So early on the morning of October 25, 1996, he went in for surgery. His doctor cut open a small part of his skull and removed the tumors. He was in surgery for six hours while his friends and family waited.

The surgery was a success. The tumors came out, and Lance's vision and coordination were not hurt. After recovering, Lance had to have more chemo. While Lance had done pretty well through his first batch[2] of chemo, this one was harsher, and it was harder on him. But it was also the critical moment in his cancer treatment. If he was going to beat the cancer, it had to be then. If the cancer didn't respond, if the chemo didn't work, Lance would almost certainly die. Time after time, Lance had gotten more and more bad news. This time, he couldn't afford anything but good news.

Lance's life revolved around his chemo. It was all he did. He was either getting a treatment or recovering from a treatment. He slept ten to twelve hours every night, his body exhausted by the battles going on inside it. He was ill, weak, and very tired. But he kept going. He told himself that the weakness and pain were signs that he was winning the battle. By the end of the treatment, all he could do was lie curled up[3] in a ball, retching[4]. He noticed brown spots on his skin—they were chemo burns. The drugs were burning his body from the inside out.

Finally, the therapy was over. Lance had to wait to find out whether the drugs had killed off the cancer. The early tests were promising. It looked like the cancer was

们真正的想法。私下里，医生们料想他活不下来。

兰斯接下来要接受脑部手术。脑部手术听起来很吓人，手术可能会破坏他的视力和他的身体协调能力。如果出问题，他将再也不能骑车了。但他别无选择，肿瘤必须被切除，他只能希望一切顺利。所以1996年10月25日，他一大早去医院做了手术。他的医生在他的头盖骨上开了一个小口，切除了肿瘤。他的手术持续了6小时，其间他的朋友和家人在外等候。

手术很成功。肿瘤被切除了，兰斯的视力和身体协调能力没有受损。恢复后，兰斯不得不接受更多的化疗。虽然兰斯的首批化疗进展顺利，但这次化疗的威力更大，他也更加痛苦。但这也是他癌症治疗的关键时刻。如果他想打败癌症，那就是现在。如果肿瘤没有反应，如果化疗不起作用，兰斯差不多一定会死。兰斯一次又一次得到越来越多的坏消息。这一次，除了好消息，他什么都承受不起了。

兰斯的生活围绕着化疗进行。这是他所做的一切。他不是接受治疗，就是从治疗中恢复。每天晚上他睡10到12个小时，他的身体因为其内部正在发生的斗争而损耗很大。他病了，身体虚弱，也很疲劳。但他坚持着。他告诉自己，虚弱和疼痛预示着他将赢得与病魔之间的战争。治疗的后期，他所能做的就是全身蜷成一团躺在床上，不断干呕。他发现皮肤上出现褐色斑点——这些是化疗灼伤的。药物从里向外灼烧着他的身体。

最终化疗结束了。兰斯必须等待结果：药物是否已经杀死了全部癌症细胞。早期的检查结果令人

[1] coordination （肌肉、动作等的）协调

[2] batch 一批

[3] curled up （身体）蜷曲

[4] retching 干呕；作呕，恶心

going away.

Lance was single-minded in beating his disease. He thought of it as a kind of race, a battle between him and cancer. "Cancer picked the wrong guy," he told a friend. "When it looked around for a body to hang out in, it made a big mistake when it chose mine."

Lance started riding his bike again. At first, he was weak. He had lost a lot of weight, most of it muscle. It was a struggle just to pedal along. But his strength slowly grew. Along with his strength grew his enthusiasm for joining the fight against cancer. He wanted to talk to other cancer patients and encourage them. He started the Lance Armstrong Foundation, based in Austin, to help fund the fight against cancer. To raise money for the foundation, he planned a charity bike race called the Ride for the Roses.

While he worked, he waited. His tests were good, and his doctors were hopeful that he would recover. But there was no way to be sure.

When Lance made a public announcement about his Ride for the Roses, he met a woman named Kristin "Kik" Richard. Richard worked in public relations and advertising. She was helping to promote the race. As Kik and Lance got to know each other better, they grew closer. Soon, they fell in love. It was an off-and-on[1] romance at first. But in time, Lance had a new partner in his struggle to gain back his old life.

乐观，看起来癌症像是消失了。

兰斯在与疾病的抗争中意志坚定：他把这看做是一场比赛，一场他与癌症之间的比赛。他对一个朋友说："癌症选错了人，它四处寻找寄身的身体，当选择了我的身体时，它犯了一个大错误。"

兰斯又开始骑车了。刚开始他很虚弱。他的体重减轻了很多，减的大部分是他的肌肉。他仅仅是踩着脚踏板缓慢骑行就非常吃力。但他的力气逐渐增长，与之伴随而来的是他加入与癌症抗争的行列的热情。他想和其他癌症患者谈心，并鼓励他们。他发起了兰斯·阿姆斯特朗基金会，基金会设在奥斯丁，旨在帮助与癌症抗争的人筹款。为了帮助基金会募集资金，他策划了一个名为玫瑰自行车赛的慈善赛事。

他工作的同时也等待着消息。检查结果很好，他的医生对他能够痊愈充满信心，但还无法肯定。

当兰斯公开宣布将举行玫瑰自行车赛时，遇上了一位名叫克丽丝汀·理查德（绰号是基克）的女人。理查德在公关和广告行业工作，她帮着推广这项比赛。随着基克和兰斯进一步了解对方，他们的关系更为亲近。不久他们相爱了。起初他们的爱情断断续续，但最终兰斯在重回原来生活的努力中有了一个新伙伴。

[1] off-and-on 断断续续的

CHAPTER SIX

BACK ON THE BIKE

重回赛场

About a year after his last chemo treatment, Lance got good news. His tests were still looking great. The doctors decided the fight was over. The cancer was gone. Lance had been cured.

It was fantastic news, putting an end to[1] a long period of anxious waiting. But Lance had a new decision to make. Would he return to cycling? Could his body possibly ever take that kind of punishment again? When Lance saw a picture of himself winning a stage at the Tour de France, he felt like that part of his life was over. He told a friend that he'd never be able to compete again. But secretly, Lance never gave up hope. He didn't say so, but he still thought of himself as a cyclist.

In the summer of 1997, Lance and Kik went to Europe. Lance got to watch the Tour de France as a spectator. He also got to tour Europe in a way he never had as a cyclist. While he often thought about racing again, he also enjoyed not having to worry about competing.

As time went on, Lance thought more and more about coming back. Chris Carmichael constantly prodded[2] him, encouraging him to start riding again. But Lance wasn't sure. Cancer and his treatment had changed him. He wasn't a strong 175 pounds anymore. Now he was a thin 158 pounds. He wouldn't have the same reserves of power that made him so fearsome[3] on the road. Still, he wanted to find a way to compete again.

Finally, he made up his mind. He was going to start training again. He wanted to return for the 1998 season. He told his team, Cofidis, that he was on his way back. But he got a surprise. The team didn't want him anymore. It canceled his contract. Cofidis didn't believe Lance would ever be the rider he had been when it

兰斯最后一次化疗大约一年后，他得到了好消息。他的检查结果依然很好，医生认定他与癌症的抗争已经结束。癌症消失了，兰斯已经痊愈。

这个消息太好了，它终结了长时间的焦急等待。但兰斯需要做出新的决定：他还要重回自行车赛场吗？他的身体还可能再次承受比赛的那种折磨吗？当兰斯看到自己赢下环法比赛一个赛段的照片时，他感到自己生命中的那个部分已经结束了。他告诉一个朋友他再也不能返回赛场了。但兰斯内心深处并没有放弃希望。他不这么说，但他依旧把自己看做一个自行车手。

1997年夏天，兰斯和基克去了欧洲。兰斯作为观众观看了环法比赛，他还以他做车手时从未有过的方式游历了欧洲。尽管他经常想重返赛场，但他也很享受不必担心比赛的感觉。

随着时间的推移，兰斯越来越想返回赛场。克里斯·卡米卡尔经常激励他重新开始比赛。但兰斯很犹豫。癌症和治疗已经改变了他，他不再是个体重175磅的强壮的人。现在他很单薄，体重158磅。他不再具有曾经使他在公路上令对手畏惧的体力储备。但他仍然想找到重回赛场的方法。

最终他打定主意，将重新开始训练。他想在1998年赛季重回赛场。他告诉他所在的科菲蒂斯车队，他要回来了。但他得到了令人吃惊的消息：车队不再想要他了，取消了他的合同。车队不相

[1] putting an end to 使……结束

[2] prodded 激励；刺激

[3] fearsome 令人畏惧的

first signed him.

At first, the situation didn't seem like a big deal. Lance had been one of the rising stars of cycling before his illness. Surely, some other team would jump at the chance to sign him. But as Lance and his agent made call after call, they started to realize something. Nobody believed Lance could come back. Nobody wanted to sign him.

Finally, Lance found someone interested. An old friend, Thomas Weisel, was running a team sponsored by the U.S. Postal Service. Weisel had once owned the Subaru-Montgomery team, which Lance had signed with years before. Weisel was willing to take a chance on the comeback. Lance signed a contact for a low salary. But the contract included incentives[1], or bonuses. If Lance performed well, he would make up for the low salary with good bonus money. If not, he'd never make much money.

After Lance signed the contract, he wanted to celebrate with the woman he loved. He could think of no better way to do that than to propose. He bought a ring and asked Kik to marry him. She agreed. They planned a wedding for May 1998.

Everything seemed to be going Lance's way. He was training hard, trying to get back into shape. In February 1998, he rode in his first professional race since he had been diagnosed with cancer. The race was the Ruta del Sol, a five-day race in Spain. Lance didn't win the race, but his fourteenth-place finish proved that he was back.

While everyone marveled at his comeback, Lance still wasn't feeling confident. He wasn't the team leader anymore. Teammate George Hincapie was the featured[2] U.S. Postal Service rider. Lance, like the other riders, was there to help Hincapie win. In his next race, called Paris-Nice for the route it runs between the

信兰斯能再次成为当初和车队签约的那个车手。

起初这个情况好像没什么大不了。兰斯生病前是自行车界的新星之一，自然会有其他车队抓住这个机会和他签约。但当兰斯和他的经纪人打了一个又一个电话后，他们开始意识到，没人相信兰斯能够找回状态，没人想签下他。

终于兰斯找到了对自己感兴趣的人。老朋友托马斯·威瑟尔正经营着一个由美国邮政局赞助的车队。威瑟尔曾是兰斯几年前签约的苏巴鲁—蒙哥马利车队的老板。威瑟尔愿意在归来的兰斯身上碰碰运气。兰斯签了一份低薪水的合同，但是合同包含激励措施，或称奖金。如果兰斯表现优异，他会得到丰厚的奖金从而弥补低薪水。如果表现不好，他将永远挣不到很多钱。

[1] incentives 鼓励；鼓励积极性的报酬（或特许）

兰斯签了合同后，想和自己所爱的女人一起庆祝。除了向她求婚，他想不出更好的庆祝方式了。他买了个戒指，请求基克嫁给自己。她同意了。他们计划在1998年5月结婚。

一切对兰斯都很顺利。他努力训练，争取重新恢复健康的体魄。1998年2月，他参加了被诊断患上癌症后的第一场职业比赛。比赛名为“太阳之路”，在西班牙举行，为期5天。兰斯没有赢得比赛，但他取得的第14名证明他回来了。

尽管每个人都惊诧于他的回归状态，兰斯依然缺乏自信。他不再是车队的领袖。队友乔治·辛卡匹是美国邮政车队的标志性车手。兰斯和其他车手一样得帮助辛卡匹获胜。兰斯参加的下场比赛是在巴黎和尼斯两座法国城市之间

[2] featured 作为号召的，作为特色的

two French cities, Lance discovered how frustrating not being the leader could be. The weather for the second stage was cold and rainy. Along the route, Hincapie had a flat tire. The entire team had to stop while he got his bike fixed. Then Lance and the other riders had to speed back to the peloton, wearing themselves out so Hincapie could save some energy.

As Lance started pedaling again, he was overcome with despair. Soon, he pulled over to the side of the road. He was done. He was quitting. And not just the race—he was quitting the entire comeback. He returned to Texas and told everyone he was retiring.

Lance's friends and family weren't sure what to do. They knew Lance wouldn't be happy if he quit. They wanted to get him back on the bike. They convinced him that he couldn't retire just yet. He had to wait until after the Ride for the Roses, his charity event. And they said he owed his U.S. fans a farewell race—the U.S. Pro Championships. Reluctantly, Lance agreed to compete in the two races. What he didn't know was that his friends and family were just stalling[1] him. They thought that in time, he would change his mind.

Chris Carmichael convinced Lance to train for the Ride for the Roses. They went to Boone, North Carolina, where Lance had twice won the Tour DuPont. There, in the Appalachian Mountains, Lance started training again. And it was there, during a long ride and final climb, that he remembered why he loved cycling. He didn't want to quit anymore. He wanted to be a cyclist again.

After his wedding in May, Lance got on his bike for the Ride for the Roses. It was a fun charity event, not a fierce professional race. Not surprisingly, Lance was the first rider across the finish line. He was ready for the U.S. Pro Championships. But it wouldn't be his farewell race, as he had once planned. It would be his second

进行的巴黎—尼斯自行车赛。兰斯发现，不当车队领袖有多么令人沮丧。在进行第2赛段的比赛时，天气寒冷，还下着雨。比赛进行中，辛卡匹的车胎爆了。在他的自行车修理期间，整个车队不得不停下来等他。然后兰斯和其他车手不得不加速赶上主车群，累得筋疲力尽，就为了让辛卡匹能够节省些体力。

当兰斯再次开始骑行时，他陷入绝望中。不久他停在了路边。他不行了。他要退出。他不仅要退出这次比赛——他还要退出整个重返赛场的计划。他回到得克萨斯州，告诉所有人他要退役。

兰斯的朋友和家人不知所措。他们知道如果兰斯退出，他并不会开心。他们想让他重回赛场。他们说服他现在还不能退休，他必须得等到他的慈善比赛——玫瑰自行车赛——之后。他们说他还欠他的美国车迷们一场告别赛——美国职业冠军赛。兰斯不情愿地同意参加上述两场比赛。他不知道他的朋友和家人只是在拖延时间。他们想，慢慢地他就会改变主意的。

[1] stalling 拖延

克里斯·卡米卡尔说服兰斯为玫瑰自行车赛训练。他们来到北卡罗来纳州的布恩，在这里兰斯曾两次赢得杜邦大奖赛的冠军。兰斯在当地的阿巴拉契亚山脉再次开始了训练。就是在那里，在一次漫长的骑行和最后的爬坡路段当中，他想起了自己热爱自行车比赛的原因。他不再想退出，他想再次成为一名自行车手。

5月份举行完婚礼后，兰斯参加了玫瑰自行车赛。这场慈善比赛很有趣，不像职业比赛那样竞争激烈。兰斯不出所料地第一个冲过终点线。他准备好参加美国职业冠军赛。但这次并非如他计划的那样是他的告别赛，这将是他第2次

return to cycling. He finished fourth (his teammate George Hincapie won) and promptly decided that it was time to move back to Europe. He and Kik packed up and moved into a house in Nice, France.

Lance got immediate results. He won the Tour of Luxembourg, a four-day race, then finished fourth at the Tour of Holland, a weeklong race. His new, thinner build and fresh determination were making him a better stage racer than he'd been before the illness. But he still didn't have the strength to compete in the 1998 Tour de France.

Lance got back on the bike for the Tour of Spain, a hard three-week race and one of cycling's toughest events. This tour was a big test—would Lance have the strength to keep up with cycling's elite[1] over such a long race? When he crossed the finish line in fourth place, a little more than 2 minutes behind winner Abraham Olano, Lance knew his body had passed the test. He was ready to become a top stage racer. A new goal emerged, one that had never really seemed possible until then. Lance wanted to win the Tour de France.

This was his focus for 1999. Everything he did was in preparation for the Tour. When Kik learned in February that she was pregnant, the goal was even clearer. Lance was going to be a father, and there was no better way to support a family than by being the best cyclist in the world.

Lance started 1999 with a thud[2], though. He crashed at the Tour of Valencia and hurt his shoulder. A few weeks later, he was hit by a car during training. He finished second in the one-day Amstel Gold Race, losing to Michael Boogerd. But even this good showing was a disappointment. Boogerd was one of the favorites to win the 1999 Tour de France. Lance had badly wanted to beat Boogerd to prove to himself that he was in the elite class.

重返自行车赛场。他取得第4名（他的队友乔治·辛卡匹夺冠），然后立即决定返回欧洲。他和基克收拾好行囊，搬进了法国尼斯的一所房子里。

兰斯很快有所斩获。他赢得了为期4天的环卢森堡自行车赛的冠军，然后在为期一周的环荷兰自行车赛中取得第4名。他更为轻盈的身体和旺盛的斗志使他成为比患病前更为优秀的赛段比赛选手。但他依然没有足够的体力参加1998年的环法自行车赛。

兰斯参加了自行车界最艰苦的比赛之一——为期3周的环西班牙自行车赛。这次比赛是一个大的考验——兰斯在这么长的比赛中有足够的体力跟上自行车高手们吗？当兰斯以比冠军亚伯拉罕·奥拉诺落后2分多钟的成绩第4个冲过终点线时，他知道他的身体已经通过了考验。他已经准备好成为一名顶尖的赛段比赛选手了。一个新的目标出现了，一个以前似乎不可能实现的目标，兰斯想成为环法自行车赛的冠军。

[1] elite　精英

这是他1999年生活的焦点，他所做的一切都是为环法比赛做准备。当基克2月份得知自己怀孕后，他的目标更明确了。兰斯要当父亲了，除了成为世界上最好的车手之外，没有更好的办法来供养一个家庭了。

[2] thud　重击

然而1999年，兰斯开局不利。他在环巴伦西亚自行车赛中发生撞车事故，肩膀受伤。几个星期后，他在训练中被一辆汽车撞了。在为期一天的阿姆斯特丹黄金赛中，他取得第2名，输给了迈克尔·博格德。即使是这样不错的表现，兰斯也感到失望。博格德是1999年环法自行车赛的夺冠热门。兰斯本来特别希望击败博格德，以此证明自己是顶尖选手。

But the disappointments didn't make him lose focus. He and the U.S. Postal Service team trained even harder. Lance turned cycling into a science. He studied hard to determine the best strategies on each stage, each type of ride. He gained back some of the weight he had lost during his cancer treatments, but he made sure he stayed lean. He carefully controlled his diet, even weighing every ounce of food he ate.

Lance couldn't know how the Tour would play out, but he could be sure of one thing. If he lost, it wouldn't be for lack of preparation.

但这种失望并没有使他失去目标。他和美国邮政车队更加刻苦地训练。兰斯把骑自行车变成了一门科学。他努力研究，确定每个赛段、每种骑行路段最好的策略。他恢复了一点癌症治疗期间减少的体重，但他确保自己保持轻盈的体态。他细心控制饮食，甚至对所吃的每一盎司的食物都要进行称重。

兰斯不知道环法比赛将如何结束，但他可以肯定一件事情，那就是如果他输了，绝不是因为准备不足。

CHAPTER **SEVEN**

COMEBACK COMPLETE

再上巅峰

Finally, July arrived. Lance and his U.S. Postal Service team were in France, ready and anxious to get started. The team's director, Johan Bruyneel, had made Lance the team leader, believing that his power gave the team the best chance for a good finish. But few cycling experts paid much attention to a team led by a cancer survivor. Most people focused on the race favorites—Abraham Olano, Michael Boogerd, Miguel Indurain, Alexander Zulle, and Bobby Julich. Only one person, former champion Miguel Indurain, mentioned Lance's name as a possible winner.

Every Tour de France opens with a short, individual time trial called the Prologue. An all-out 8-kilometer (5-mile) sprint, the trial is important for the contenders. Nobody wants to get off to a poor start. The Tour is long and grueling enough without having to start out from behind.

As riders took off, the weather was perfect for racing. It didn't take long before Olano broke the Prologue record of 8:12 by 1 second. Shortly after that, Zulle broke the new record with a time of 8:07. Lance just wanted to stay with the lead group. As he crossed the finish line, he looked up at the clock. He was shocked by what he saw: 8:02—five seconds faster than Zulle and better than the old record by 10 seconds. For the first time in his life, he had earned the yellow jersey. The twenty-seven-year-old American was leading the Tour de France. He could hardly believe it.

Lance held on to the yellow jersey through stage 1 but lost it to Estonia's Jaan Kirsipuu the next day. He wasn't worried, though. The early stages of the Tour are in some ways just a warm-up for the brutal climbing stages at the end. The first part of the race takes place mainly on

7月最终到来了。兰斯和美国邮政车队来到法国，他们做好了准备，焦急地等待比赛开始。车队经理乔汉·布鲁尼尔已经让兰斯成为车队领袖，相信他的力量使车队最有希望取得好成绩。但在自行车比赛专家中，几乎没人注意到这支由癌症康复者领军的车队。大多数人把目光投向了那些热门选手——亚伯拉罕·奥拉诺、迈克尔·博格德、米盖尔·安杜兰、亚历山大·祖尔和鲍比·朱利奇。只有前环法比赛冠军米盖尔·安杜兰一人提到兰斯有可能获胜。

每次环法自行车赛都是以一个短距离个人计时赛作为开幕赛。这个计时赛总长8公里（5英里），选手们在比赛中会竭尽全力冲刺。这场比赛对每个参赛选手都很重要。环法比赛已经够长、够艰苦了，没人想开局不利，一开始就落后。

选手们出发时，天气非常适合比赛。没过多久，奥拉诺就以1秒的优势打破了开幕赛的比赛纪录——8分12秒。很快，祖尔又以8分7秒的成绩打破了新纪录。兰斯只想着和领先的选手们并驾齐驱。当他冲过终点线时，他抬头看了看表。当他看到8分2秒时，他惊呆了——他比祖尔快了5秒，比原来的比赛纪录快了10秒。兰斯一生中第一次获得了黄色领骑衫。这位27岁的美国人成为了环法比赛的领骑车手，他简直不敢相信。

兰斯在第1赛段保住了黄色领骑衫，但第2天他把它输给了爱沙尼亚的贾恩·基尔斯普乌。他并不担心。从某种意义上说，环法比赛的开始阶段只是比赛后段残酷的爬坡赛段的热身。比赛前段主要在

flat roads, which favor sprinters. But sprinters often fade during the climbing stages. All Lance had to do was stay with the leaders. His team rode in front of him, blocking the wind and giving him a good draft. They helped him stay up front without using up his legs too early.

During stage 2, a big crash slowed down many of the Tour's top contenders, including Boogerd and Zulle. Lance was in front of the mess. As the riders behind him slowed, he gained a big cushion[1] over many of his most serious rivals.

Over the next week, Lance and his team did what they could to stay near the front. Lance didn't care too much about leading. He was saving his legs for the climbs. But by stage 8, he was ready to make a move. This 56.5-kilometer (35-mile) time trial around the city of Metz would be a great chance to make up time. Stage 8 also included two tough climbs, and Lance was eager to prove that he was a complete rider.

Lance started his time trial 2 minutes after Abraham Olano. When his turn to start finally came, he pedaled hard. He wanted to catch Olano and shake the Spaniard's confidence. This goal didn't take long to achieve. Early in the race, Olano crashed and lost a little time. Then Lance was on him. He blew by Olano, who had never before been passed in a time trial.

Lance was thrilled. But he wasn't done yet. He continued to stomp down on the pedals, putting up times that blew away the entire field. By the time he crossed the finish line, he had built a big lead, beating second-place Zulle by almost a minute. The yellow jersey was his again, and this time, he didn't want to give it back.

Overall, the win gave Lance a lead of 2:20 over second-place Christophe Moreau of France. But Moreau

平地进行，这对冲刺型选手有利。但冲刺型选手经常在爬坡赛段落后。兰斯所要做的就是和领先的选手们并驾齐驱。他的队友骑在他前面，替他挡风，让他“搭顺风车”，帮助他骑在车群前部，而他的腿也不会太早疲劳。

在第2赛段，一场大的撞车事故延缓了包括博格德和祖尔在内的很多赛事顶尖选手的前进速度。兰斯在事故现场的前面，当他后面的选手慢下来的时候，他和许多他最大的竞争对手之间就有了一个很大的缓冲。

[1] cushion 缓冲

在接下来的一个星期，兰斯和队友尽其所能保持在车群的前部。兰斯不太关心是否骑在最前面，他在为爬坡赛段节省腿部力量。但是到了第8赛段，他准备行动了。这是个环绕梅兹城全长56.5公里（35英里）的计时赛，它是弥补他和其他选手之间的时间差距的好机会。第8赛段也包括两个艰苦的爬坡路段，兰斯渴望证明自己是个全面的车手。

兰斯在亚伯拉罕·奥拉诺出发2分钟之后出发。当最终他的出发时间到来时，他开始奋力蹬脚踏板。他想赶上奥拉诺，动摇这个西班牙人的信心。没过多久，这个目标就实现了。在比赛开始阶段，奥拉诺发生撞车事故，延误了一点时间。兰斯追上了奥拉诺，从他身旁呼啸而过，而在此之前他还从未在计时赛中被人赶超。

兰斯高兴坏了，但他没有就此打住。他继续猛蹬脚踏板，取得了时间上的优势，大败全场选手。当他冲过终点线时，他已经确立了很大的领先优势，比第2名祖尔领先了将近1分钟。他夺回了黄色领骑衫，而这次，他不想再让给任何人。

总的来说，这场胜利使兰斯领先第2名——法国车手克里斯多夫·莫罗——2分20秒。但是莫罗并

wasn't a strong climber. The next real threat was Olano, 2:33 behind. A day off after the time trial allowed Lance to enjoy his lead. But he knew there was a lot of work to do. Stage 9 was the beginning of the true climbing stages. It was a 132-kilometer (82-mile) ride across six mountain passes. Many experts expected Lance to fade in the mountains. Early in his career, the climbs had been tough on him. Experts thought a more complete rider would catch him.

Lance wasted little time in proving that he wasn't going away. He worked with his teammates to draft throughout the early parts of the stage, saving his legs for a late attack. Soon, the weather turned cold, and rain began to fall. As the riders descended a peak, hailstones[1] battered down on them. Several of Lance's teammates slowed. Another one crashed. Soon, Lance was without any help, riding with the world's best climbers. He fell behind the lead group. But he never let up[2]. Alone, with nobody to turn to, Lance did the only thing he could think of—he attacked.

With 8 kilometers (5 miles) to go, Lance stood up and started pumping the pedals. After a half mile or so, he was within 10 seconds of the leaders. Once he could see them, he worked even harder. They looked back and saw the yellow jersey coming up fast. Still attacking, Lance sailed by and took the stage lead.

He kept going, wondering if the others had enough energy left to keep up. He wanted to crush their hopes, to show them they had no chance of catching him. His plan worked. The other riders couldn't match his pace. He pulled away, alone. Soon, no other riders were within sight. He crossed the finish line all by himself for a second straight stage win. More important, his lead over Olano had grown to an amazing 6 minutes.

Despite his great success, Lance still had his critics[3]. Reporters questioned how a man who had been a cancer

不是优秀的爬坡选手，下一个真正的威胁是落后2分33秒的奥拉诺。计时赛后休息一天，兰斯可以享受领先带来的快乐。但他知道还有很多事情要做。第9赛段是真正的爬坡赛段的开始，这个赛段全长132公里（82英里），要穿越6个山口。许多专家预测，兰斯会在山区落在车群后面。在他职业生涯早期，爬坡赛段对他而言非常严酷。专家们认为一个更全面的车手将赶上兰斯。

兰斯很快证明自己不会落在后面。赛段开始阶段，他骑在队友后面，为后面的冲刺节省腿部力量。不久，天气转冷，开始下雨。当选手们从一个山顶下来时，下起了冰雹。兰斯的好几个队友慢下来，另外一个发生撞车事故。很快兰斯便失去了任何帮手，和世界上最好的爬坡选手一起竞争。他落在领先的选手后面，但他没有松劲。独自一人，没有帮手可以依靠的兰斯做了他唯一能想到的——冲刺。

[1] hailstones 冰雹

[2] let up 放松；减弱

赛段还剩下8公里（5英里），兰斯从车座上站起来，开始用力蹬脚踏板。前进大约半英里后，他和领先选手们的差距缩短到10秒内。一旦他能看到他们，他就更加努力了。领先选手们向后看，见到了黄色领骑衫的拥有者快速赶上来。兰斯一直冲刺，快速超过这些选手，取得了赛段的领先。

他继续前进，不知道其他选手是否有足够的体力赶上来。他想使他们的希望破灭，向他们证明他们不可能赶上他的速度。他的计划奏效了，其他选手赶不上他的速度。他独自脱离了车群。很快，他再也看不到其他选手。他独自冲过终点线，取得连续第2个赛段胜利。更为重要的是，他对奥拉诺的领先优势增加到令人惊讶的6分钟。

尽管取得了巨大成功，兰斯依然还有批评者。记者们对一个几年前还是癌症患者的人在这样艰苦的体

[3] critics 批评挑剔的人；评论家

patient only a few years before could possibly be leading such a grueling sporting event. He had never been a contender before the cancer, the critics noted. Why was he so good all of a sudden? Some people suspected that Lance was doping[1]—using steroids[2] or other performance-enhancing drugs. Lance told his critics that he had never used illegal drugs. Every drug test proved that he was "clean"—or drug free.

For the rest of the Tour, Lance's huge lead was a big advantage. He didn't really need to attack anymore. He just had to stay with the peloton and not let anyone jump out too far ahead. By the end of stage 13, his lead was 7:44. He continued his conservative[3] approach, just riding along and staying out of trouble.

At the end of stage 15, Lance was riding at the front with Spaniard Fernando Escartín. The stage ran along France's border with Spain, so Escartín badly wanted to win. The Spaniard attacked hard, quickly pulling away from Lance. Lance could have tried to keep up, but he didn't *have* to keep up. He crossed the finish line more than 2 minutes behind Escartín. Even so, Lance wasn't worried. Escartín had moved into second place overall, but he was still a whopping[4] 6:19 behind Lance.

By this time, the rest of the Tour was a formality[5]. "Armstrong is the strongest. He's going to win the Tour, no question," said Alexander Zulle. "He is in control over every situation....It's been like that for two weeks."

Lance had one more goal. The Tour includes three individual time trials. Lance had won the first two. Only three riders had ever won all three. Lance wanted to match their feat[6] by winning stage 19 on the second-to-last day of the Tour. Some people advised him to take it easy, not to push. But his mind was made up. He was going for the sweep[7]. "The time trials are...the race of truth," he said. "It would have been easy to go 90

育赛事中领先表示怀疑。批评者注意到兰斯在患癌症前从来都不是环法比赛的冠军争夺者。为什么忽然之间他就如此优秀？一些人怀疑兰斯在服药——服用类固醇或其他提高比赛成绩的药物。兰斯告诉他的批评者，他从未使用违禁药物。每次药检都证明他是“干净”的——没有服药。

在接下来的比赛中，兰斯巨大的领先是一大优势。他不再需要去冲刺。他只要跟着主车群，不让任何人领先太多。第13赛段结束，他领先7分44秒。他继续采用保守战术，避开麻烦。

在第15赛段，兰斯和西班牙人费尔南多·埃斯卡廷一起骑在车群前部。这个赛段在法国和西班牙交界处进行，所以埃斯卡廷非常想赢。这个西班牙人猛烈冲刺，很快甩开了兰斯。兰斯本可以努力赶上，但他不必这么做。他以落后埃斯卡廷2分多钟的成绩第2个冲过终点线。即使这样，兰斯并不担心。埃斯卡廷的总成绩已经排在第2位，但他仍然远远落后兰斯达6分19秒。

到这个时候，剩下的比赛只是个形式了。亚历山大·祖尔说：“阿姆斯特朗是最强的。他将毫无疑问地赢得环法比赛的胜利。他在每种形势下都操控着比赛……这种情况持续了两个星期。”

兰斯还有一个目标。环法比赛包括3个个人计时赛，兰斯赢下了前两个。只有3位选手曾经赢下全部3个计时赛。兰斯想赢下环法比赛倒数第2天举行的第19赛段，从而赶上那3位选手的成就。一些人建议他放松点，不要冲刺。但他下决心了，他要大获全胜。他说：“计时赛是……真正的竞赛。

[1] doping 服用麻醉品（或毒品）

[2] steroids 类固醇

[3] conservative 保守的；谨慎的

[4] whopping 巨大的

[5] formality 俗套；仪式；（无实际意义的）形式性手续

[6] feat 功绩；壮举

[7] sweep （比赛等的）全胜，全赢

percent, but I wanted to prove the [rider with the] yellow jersey is the strongest one in the race."

Lance started off fast, with the best time at each of the first two checkpoints. But as he approached the end of the 57-kilometer (35-mile) course, his legs grew tired. Despite his aching muscles, he pedaled harder, faster. He crossed the finish line with a time of 1:08:17—9 seconds better than second-place Zulle. Lance had done it—he had won stage 19 and swept the time trials. It was his way of putting an exclamation point on his Tour win.

The final day, stage 20, was almost like a celebration parade for Lance. By tradition, the peloton doesn't do any real racing during most of the 89-kilometer (55-mile) stage. They don't start riding fast until they see the famous Eiffel Tower[1] of Paris. Lance was relaxed as he rode. He did interviews through his radio headset. He even ate an ice cream cone on his bike.

As he pedaled over the cobblestones[2] of a street called the Champs-Elysées, the crowd cheered. Spectators waved Texan and American flags all along the course. After he crossed the finish line as the winner, Lance ran to hug Kik and his mom. He was overjoyed. He had accomplished what had seemed almost impossible—he had beaten cancer and returned to cycling as a better racer than he had been before the illness. "This is an awesome day," he said. "This is beyond belief."

Even though most Americans don't follow cycling, Lance was an instant hit back in the United States. His good looks and positive attitude, along with his inspirational victory over cancer, made him an irresistible story. He was in high demand, appearing on *Late Night with David Letterman, Today, Larry King Live*, and other TV shows. New sponsors wanted to sign

取得90%的胜利很容易，但我想证明黄色领骑衫（车手）是比赛的最强者。”

兰斯一开始速度很快，在前两个检查站都取得了最好成绩。但当他接近57公里（35英里）长的赛道末尾时，他的双腿变得疲劳。尽管肌肉疼痛，他越骑越猛，越骑越快。他以1小时8分17秒的成绩冲过终点线——比第2名祖尔快了9秒。兰斯做到了——他赢下了第19赛段，在计时赛大获全胜。他用这样的方式给他环法比赛的胜利画上了一个惊叹号。

最后一天第20赛段的比赛对兰斯而言就像是庆祝游行。传统上，选手们在89公里（55英里）长的比赛中的大部分时间不会真正地竞争，直到看到巴黎著名的埃菲尔铁塔，他们才开始快速骑行。兰斯在骑行过程中很放松，他通过头戴式受话器接受采访，他甚至在自行车上吃了一个冰淇淋蛋卷。

当他骑行在由鹅卵石铺就的香榭丽舍大街上时，人群一片欢呼。赛道旁的观众挥舞着得克萨斯州州旗和美国国旗。兰斯作为胜利者冲过终点线后，跑向基克和妈妈并拥抱了她们。他太高兴了。他取得了似乎不可能取得的胜利——他打败了癌症，然后作为比病前更为优秀的车手重返自行车赛场。他说：“这是美好的一天，令人难以置信。”

尽管大多数美国人不喜欢自行车比赛，兰斯还是迅速在美国成为热点人物。他英俊的外表，积极的态度，还有他令人鼓舞的对抗癌症的胜利，使他的故事令人难以抗拒。他极受欢迎，出现在《大卫·莱特曼的午夜漫谈》、《今天》、《拉里·金现场》和其他美国电视节目中。新的赞助商想和他签订

[1] Eiffel Tower
埃菲尔铁塔（法国巴黎著名景点之一）

[2] cobblestones
圆石，卵石

him to endorsement[1] deals. He agreed to write an autobiography. Everybody wanted a piece of Lance Armstrong.

The good news kept coming. That October, Lance was giving a speech in Las Vegas[2], Nevada, when he got a phone call from Kik. She told him she was going into labor, the beginning stages of having their baby. Lance was surprised. She wasn't due to give birth for two more weeks. But he quickly got on a flight back home. After a difficult delivery, Luke David Armstrong was born on October 12, 1999. Lance and Kik were parents.

Everything was going perfectly. Lance had conquered his past. In the present, he was the world's best cyclist. And his future seemed secure with his infant son.

[1] endorsement 赞同，支持；担保

[2] Las Vegas 拉斯维加斯(美国最大的赌城和娱乐城)

广告合同。他同意写本自传。兰斯·阿姆斯特朗很受大家欢迎。

好消息接踵而至。那年10月，兰斯正在内华达州的拉斯维加斯演讲时接到了基克的电话，她告诉他，自己即将分娩，也就是生孩子的开始阶段。兰斯很吃惊。她本来要两个多星期后才生产的。但他很快坐上回家的飞机。1999年10月12日，艰难的分娩之后，卢克·大卫·阿姆斯特朗出生了。兰斯和基克成了父母亲。

一切都很完美。兰斯战胜了过去。现在他是世界上最好的自行车手，对于有了儿子的他，未来显得无忧无虑。

CHAPTER EIGHT

DEFENDING THE TITLE

卫冕冠军

Despite all his success, Lance still felt he had something to prove. Some experts in the cycling world discounted[1] his 1999 Tour victory. They thought his victory might be a fluke[2]—a stroke of luck—and that he could never repeat it. They pointed out that 1997 champion Jan Ullrich and 1998 champion Marco Pantani had missed the 1999 Tour and how they might have beaten Lance if they'd been there.

To counter the criticism, Lance focused only on the Tour. All the other races faded in importance for him. They were just warm-ups. All that mattered was the Tour de France and proving that his win hadn't been a fluke.

Doubt about Lance's ability to repeat only grew in the spring of 2000. He was practicing with the U.S. Postal Service team on a hot day in the Pyrenees. As Lance sped down a slope, he hit a small rock that blew out his front tire. He lost control of the bike and sailed into a brick wall that ran alongside the road. He hit the wall headfirst and briefly lost consciousness.

It was a violent and terrifying crash. Lance's teammates rushed to help their leader. But Lance had a bit of very good luck on his side. Two tourists had been sitting nearby. Both of them were doctors. They rushed to his side. "From the sound of his head hitting the wall, I was 100 percent sure I would walk over here and find a dead man," said one of the doctors.

Lance wasn't dead, though. He was rushed to the nearest hospital, treated, and released. He was banged up and bruised, but that was all. He'd be all right. After a few days' rest, he was back on the bike, training again. By the time July came, he was ready.

[1] discounted 不予重视；不全信；将信将疑
[2] fluke 侥幸

尽管取得了这一切成绩，兰斯依然觉得他需要证明自己。自行车界的一些专家对他在1999年取得的环法比赛胜利将信将疑。他们认为他获胜可能是因为侥幸——走了好运——他不可能再次夺冠。他们指出，1997年环法冠军扬·乌尔里希和1998年冠军马科·潘塔尼没有参加1999年环法比赛，如果他们在，他们将击败兰斯。

为了反击对他的批评，兰斯只专注于环法比赛，所有其他比赛对他来说都不再重要，它们只是热身而已。重要的是环法比赛，重要的是证明自己的获胜并非侥幸。

2000年春天，人们对兰斯是否具备再次夺冠的能力产生了更大的怀疑。在天气非常炎热的一天，兰斯正与美国邮政车队的队友一起在比利牛斯山脉训练。当兰斯快速冲下一个斜坡时，他的自行车撞到了一小块岩石，前胎爆了。他的自行车失去了控制，撞上了公路旁的一堵砖墙。他的头部最先撞墙，暂时失去了意识。

撞击非常猛烈，令人恐惧。兰斯的队友冲上前去救助他们的领袖。但兰斯有好运相伴。两个游客当时坐在旁边，他们都是医生。他们冲到了兰斯旁边，其中一位医生说："根据他头部撞墙的声音，我百分之百肯定，我走过来时将发现一具尸体。"

但兰斯没死。他被迅速送到最近的一家医院，接受了治疗，然后出院。他的身体撞伤并且擦伤，但也仅限于此。他会好起来的。休息了几天之后，他又开始骑车训练了。到7月份的时候，他已经做好了准备。

The 2000 Tour de France would be very different from the race Lance had won the year before. The competitors—including Ullrich and Pantani—would be tougher. The course would be different and more difficult. Race officials had decided to have the course run counterclockwise[1], the opposite direction of the previous year. The new direction created some very difficult stages.

Lance got an immediate reminder that repeating wouldn't be easy. He finished second in the opening, 16-kilometer (10-mile) time trial. He was only 2 seconds behind leader David Millar, but Lance knew he had work to do.

Through the early stages, Lance and his teammates just tried to stay in the pack. They were confident that they could build a lead in the mountains. The goal early on was to stay out of trouble and avoid crashes. By the end of stage 9, Lance was in sixteenth place.

Stage 10—in the Pyrenees—was where the race would really begin for Lance. The stage included a brutal 13-kilometer (8-mile) climb. Lance knew the climb would bury most of the riders in front of him. He got on his bike on a cold and windy morning knowing that this was his day to claim the yellow jersey.

Early in the stage, Spaniard Javier Otxoa began an attack. It was a bizarre[2] move, far too early in the race. But Otxoa built a huge lead, leaving Lance and the other riders wondering what to do. They decided to let him go. As Lance approached the long climb, he stayed in a pack with Zulle, Ullrich, and Pantani.

Not long into the climb, Pantani attacked. But Lance wouldn't let him go. He stayed on the Italian's back wheel, not giving up an inch. While the others tired, Lance kept attacking. Soon, he was behind only Otxoa. With 5 kilometers (3 miles) to go, Lance was 5 minutes behind

[1] counterclockwise 逆时针方向地

[2] bizarre 怪异的，异乎寻常的

2000年环法比赛与兰斯夺冠的1999年环法比赛迥然不同。竞争对手——包括乌尔里希和潘塔尼——将更加难对付。比赛路线改变了，而且更加艰苦。赛事官员决定按逆时针方向设定比赛路线，也就是和去年的比赛路线正好相反。新的比赛路线带来了很多非常艰苦的赛段。

兰斯立刻意识到再次夺冠将非常艰难。在开幕赛——16公里（10英里）长的计时赛中，他取得第2名，只比领先者大卫·米勒慢了2秒，但兰斯知道他得加把劲了。

在比赛开始阶段，兰斯和队友只是努力跟上车群，他们有自信可以在山区确立领先优势。开始的目标就是避免撞车，远离麻烦。到第9赛段结束，兰斯排名第16位。

第10赛段在比利牛斯山脉中进行，对于兰斯而言这是比赛真正的开始。这个赛段包括一段艰苦的长达13公里（8英里）的爬坡路段。兰斯知道这个坡路将葬送他前面的大部分车手。在寒冷而多风的早晨，兰斯跨上赛车，他知道今天该是夺回黄色领骑衫的时候了。

比赛一开始，西班牙选手贾维尔·奥祖亚开始冲刺。这个举动显得很怪异，因为为时尚早。但奥祖亚确立了很大的领先优势，使兰斯和其他选手不知如何应对。他们决定随他去。在兰斯接近坡路的过程中，他与祖尔、乌尔里希和潘塔尼保持一致。

刚进入坡路，潘塔尼就开始冲刺了，但兰斯不会让他甩开自己。他紧跟在这个意大利人的自行车后轮后面，寸步不离。其他选手都累了，兰斯依然在冲刺。很快，他前面只剩奥祖亚了。当比赛还剩下5公里（3英里）时，兰斯落后这个西班牙人

the Spaniard. With 2 kilometers (1.2 miles) left, Lance had cut the lead to just over 2 minutes. Otxoa was tired.

Lance kept attacking, hoping he could make up the time. But Otxoa had enough energy to hold off the American and win the stage. Lance was disappointed not to get the stage win. It was still a good day, though. He'd beaten his serious rivals and pulled into the overall lead, earning the yellow jersey for the first time since riding into Paris the year before.

The lead continued to grow in the mountains. The only real trouble Lance had came at the end of stage 12, at Mont Ventoux. He was riding at the front of the pack with Pantani. The two cyclists were battling for the stage lead. But shortly before the finish line, Lance stopped his attack. He was confident in his overall lead, so he let Pantani win the stage.

His decision angered Pantani. He thought Lance was just showing off by letting someone else win. "I don't need to be given a gift from Armstrong," Pantani said. "The Tour is not over. If Armstrong thinks it's finished, he's mistaken. In any case he isn't finished with me."

By stage 16, even Pantani knew that he wouldn't catch Lance. So he took out his anger in a different way—by trying to wear out the twenty-eight-year-old Texan. Pantani made an early attack and built a huge stage lead. He wasn't trying to win, though. He knew that as the leader, Lance would have to try to keep up. Pantani just wanted to wear Lance down so other riders could gain time. His plan worked—both riders ran out of energy before the end of the stage. The peloton passed them, and Lance lost more than a minute and a half of his lead to Ullrich. After the stage, Pantani withdrew from the race.

In the end, Pantani's attack didn't really hurt Lance. He quickly built his lead back and showed that nobody

5分钟。比赛还剩下2公里（1.2英里）时，兰斯又把差距缩短到2分钟多一点。奥祖亚累了。

兰斯继续冲刺，希望能弥补落后的时间。但是奥祖亚有足够的体力甩开这个美国人，并且赢下了这个赛段。没有赢下这个赛段的兰斯很失望，但那天还不错。他已打败了对他最有威胁的对手，在总成绩上取得领先，在上一年进入巴黎赛段之后第一次赢得了黄色领骑衫。

他的领先优势在山路上不断扩大。在旺图山进行的第12赛段的末尾，兰斯遇到了唯一的真正的困难。他和潘塔尼骑在队伍前面，两人争夺领先者的位置。快到终点线时，兰斯停止了冲刺。他对自己总成绩上的领先优势很自信，所以他让潘塔尼赢了这个赛段。

他的决定激怒了潘塔尼，他认为兰斯让别人赢是在炫耀自己。潘塔尼说："我不需要阿姆斯特朗送我礼物。环法比赛还没有结束。如果阿姆斯特朗认为比赛已经结束，他就错了。不管怎么样，我们两个之间还没有结束。"

到了第16赛段，潘塔尼自己也知道他不可能赶上兰斯，所以他用另外一种方式——拖垮这个28岁的得州人——释放自己的愤怒。潘塔尼很早就开始冲刺，确立了很大的领先优势，但他不打算赢。他知道作为领先选手的兰斯必须跟上他。潘塔尼就是想拖垮兰斯，这样其他选手就可以赢得时间。他的计划奏效了——赛段还没结束，他和兰斯就没力气了。主车群超过了他俩，兰斯对乌尔里希的领先优势减少了超过一分半钟。这个赛段结束后，潘塔尼退出了比赛。

最终，潘塔尼的冲刺并没有伤害到兰斯。他很快重新确立了领先优势，证明无人能赶上自己。到了第

was going to catch him. By stage 19, a time trial, only one goal remained. Lance wanted to win a stage. Despite his comfortable lead, he hadn't done that yet in 2000.

Ullrich, still in second place, started the time trial 3 minutes before Lance. Ullrich was a big crowd favorite because the stage went through part of his home country of Germany. Fans also wanted to see him cut into Lance's lead to make the final stages more interesting. But at each checkpoint, Lance's times were better. He wasn't going to lose ground[1] to Ullrich. He crossed the finish line 25 seconds faster than his rival to earn the stage win and increase his overall lead to more than 6 minutes.

"I really wanted to win this stage," he said. "I had a lot of stress and a lot of anger and a lot of pressure. The Tour wouldn't be complete for me ... without winning a stage."

Again, the final stages were just a formality. Lance rode across the finish line of stage 21 in Paris with a glass of champagne in his hand. When the race was over, he stood on the podium with Kik and nine-month-old Luke. "This one's even more special than last year, partly because of this little guy," Lance said, holding Luke.

Lance didn't spend much time celebrating. He needed to prepare for his next big race, at the 2000 Olympics in Sydney, Australia. He had been disappointed with both of his Olympic finishes before. This time, he wanted gold.

But again, a crash in training hurt his chances. Riding around a sharp turn, Lance ran into a car. He flew off his bike headfirst, onto the ground. The next day, he went to a doctor, who told him he'd broken a bone in his neck.

Lance rested for a few days, then got back to training. The injury was painful, but Lance stayed in shape. By the time he got to Sydney, he was well enough to compete.

19赛段——一个计时赛——他的目标只剩下一个：赢下这个赛段。尽管他的领先优势很大，但他在2000年的比赛中还没有赢下一个赛段。

总成绩排在第2位的乌尔里希比兰斯早3分钟开始计时赛。乌尔里希很受观众欢迎，因为这个赛段经过他的祖国德国的部分区域。车迷们也希望看到他缩短与兰斯的差距，使最后几个赛段更加有趣。但是在每个检查站，兰斯的成绩都比乌尔里希好。兰斯面对乌尔里希不准备退却。他冲过终点线，比对手的成绩快了25秒，赢下了这个赛段，同时把领先优势扩大到超过6分钟。

[1] lose ground 后退；退却；失利

他说："我真的想赢下这个赛段。我心中充满了紧张、愤怒和压力。环法比赛对我将是不完整的……如果不赢下一个赛段。"

最后的赛段又一次成了形式。在巴黎进行的第21赛段，兰斯手里拿着一杯香槟骑过了终点线。比赛结束时，他与基克和9个月大的卢克一起站在了领奖台上。兰斯抱着卢克说："今年比去年更加特殊，部分原因就是这个小家伙。"

兰斯没有花多少时间庆祝，他需要去准备下一个大赛——2000年澳大利亚悉尼奥运会。他对前两次奥运会的比赛成绩很失望，这一次，他想要金牌。

但是训练中的一次撞车事故又一次毁掉了他的夺冠机会。兰斯在骑过一个急转弯时，撞到了一辆汽车。他飞离了赛车，头先撞在地上。第2天，他去看医生，医生说他颈部的一块骨头断了。

兰斯休息了几天，然后重新开始训练。受伤部位很疼，但兰斯保持着良好状态。当他抵达悉尼的时候，他的康复情况足以使他参加比赛了。

But he still wasn't 100 percent, and it showed. He took thirteenth place in the road race event and third in the time trial. Third place got him a bronze medal, but Lance was disappointed. He'd had his heart set on gold.

Lance's life didn't get any easier in November 2000. On Thanksgiving Day, French officials announced that they were launching a criminal investigation into Lance—and his U.S. Postal Service teammates—for illegal drug use. Lance was absolutely shocked. The only evidence the French officials had was a bag of garbage that team doctors had thrown away. Because the garbage hadn't been disposed of in the usual place, investigators suspected that it contained something the team didn't want found.

The team denied all the reports. Lance insisted that he'd never used performance-enhancing drugs. He said the idea was absurd[1]—that he would never risk his health by using dangerous drugs after fighting so hard for his life only a few years earlier. But the rumors only grew more widespread. To make matters worse, Greg LeMond, the most successful American cyclist, publicly criticized Lance, suggesting that the drug use accusations were true. LeMond's remarks hurt Lance.

Life in France became increasingly difficult. The French fans had never really liked Lance in the first place. They considered cycling their sport, and they didn't want Americans coming in and dominating it. On top of that, the scandal was everywhere. The media constantly hung out around Lance's home in Nice, even when he was off training and Kik was there alone. Reporters dug through his garbage, hoping to find some evidence of guilt. Soon, Lance couldn't take it anymore. He and Kik moved to nearby Girona, Spain.

But it wasn't just the media causing problems.

但他还没有百分之百恢复，这个情况在比赛中显现出来。他在公路赛中取得第13名，计时赛中取得第3名。第3名的成绩为他赢得了一枚铜牌，但兰斯很失望。他本来是冲着金牌来的。

2000年11月，兰斯的生活并没有变得轻松。在感恩节那天，法国官员宣布他们将展开针对兰斯——和他所在的美国邮政车队——使用违禁药物的犯罪调查。兰斯十分震惊。法国官员拥有的唯一证据是队医丢弃的一袋垃圾。因为垃圾没有被丢弃在通常存放垃圾的地方，所以调查人员怀疑袋子里藏有美国邮政车队不想被人发现的东西。

车队否认了所有的报道。兰斯坚称没有使用提高成绩的药物。他说，认为他使用违禁药物的想法非常荒谬——他几年前还在为生命努力抗争，所以永远不会冒着损害健康的危险使用危险的药物。但是谣言散布得越来越广。雪上加霜的是，美国最成功的自行车手格雷格·勒芒公开批评兰斯，并暗示针对他使用违禁药物的指控属实。勒芒的言论伤害了兰斯。

[1] absurd 荒谬的

在法国的生活越来越不好过。法国的车迷一开始就从未真正喜欢过兰斯。他们把自行车看做是他们的运动，不想让美国人加入并主宰自行车比赛。除此之外，到处都是谣言。媒体总是徘徊在兰斯在尼斯的家的附近，甚至在他外出训练而基克独自一人在家时也是如此。记者在他家的垃圾中翻找，希望发现一些犯罪证据。很快，兰斯无法再忍受，他和基克搬到了附近的西班牙赫罗纳。

但是不仅仅是媒体在制造麻烦。赞助商开

Sponsors began to back away from Lance and his teammates. They didn't want to be associated with any athletes that were thought of as cheaters. It didn't matter that there was no proof. Many people had already made up their minds that Lance was guilty.

The French courts requested all the urine samples[1] that Lance had provided for earlier drug tests. The court's scientists checked the samples over and over, searching for proof of drug use. They could never find any. But the scientists still wouldn't clear Lance's name. They checked the samples again. The investigation dragged on and on. In the end, the court decided what Lance knew all along. There was no proof Lance had done anything wrong.

In April 2001, Lance and Kik got some much-needed good news. Kik was pregnant again. The couple later learned that she would have twins. The family was growing fast.

Things got even better in July, when Lance staged his amazing come-from-behind victory in the 2001 Tour de France, erasing[2] a 35-minute deficit[3] in only a few days. It was an extra-special win for Lance because he wanted to make a statement to the fans and race officials who had doubted him during the doping investigation. Lance was a three-time Tour champion and the best stage racer in the world. How long could he keep going? Only Lance could answer that question.

始远离兰斯和他的队友。他们不想和任何被认为是作弊者的运动员扯上关系。没有证据并不重要，很多人已经认定兰斯是有罪的。

法国法庭要求得到兰斯先前为药检提供的所有尿液样本。法庭的科学家反复检查样本，搜寻使用违禁药物的证据。他们永远也无法找到任何证据，但是他们仍然不洗刷兰斯的罪名。他们再次检查了样本。调查一拖再拖。最后法庭裁定没有证据证明兰斯做错了什么，而这一点兰斯始终很清楚。

2001年4月，兰斯和基克得到了非常渴望的好消息：基克又怀孕了。后来他俩得知她怀的是双胞胎。他们的家庭急速扩大。

7月，事情变得越来越好，兰斯在2001年环法比赛中几天内就消除了35分钟的落后差距，上演了惊人的后来居上的胜利。这次获胜对兰斯而言非常特殊，因为他想对在禁药调查中怀疑过他的车迷和赛事官员公开宣示。兰斯是环法比赛的三冠王，是世界上最好的赛段车手。他还能走多远？只有兰斯能回答这个问题。

[1] urine samples 尿样

[2] erasing 消除；擦去

[3] deficit 落后，失利

CHAPTER NINE

CYCLING LEGEND

传奇车手

After his recovery, Lance worried whether the cancer was really gone from his body. He lived in fear that the disease would come back. In October 2001, a few months after his third-straight Tour victory, Lance made a trip to his doctor for tests. It was the five-year anniversary of his cancer diagnosis—a major date for a cancer survivor. If cancer hasn't returned after five years, doctors consider the patient to be completely cancer free. Lance got that news from his doctor. The cancer was gone, and it wasn't likely to ever come back.

More good news came in November when Kik gave birth to twin girls, Isabelle and Grace. Everything seemed perfect. But with three small children and a busy cycling schedule, Lance and Kik had difficulty making time for themselves. They didn't talk as much anymore. They were both so wrapped up in[1] their lives that they began to grow apart.

Lance was growing even closer to his teammates, however. The U.S. Postal Service team had earned the nickname Big Blue for the blue jerseys the team members wore. Lance's three straight Tour wins had made the once little-known team into a powerhouse[2]. He was surrounded by good teammates—cyclists who knew what it took to work as a team. They were willing to work and sweat to give their leader any advantage.

Their dedication to Lance and to the team showed again in the 2002 Tour. Lance was trying to become only the fourth rider in Tour history to win a fourth-straight title. If he could do it, he would join an elite list of riders—Jacques Anquetil, Eddy Merckx, and Miguel Indurain.

The 2002 Tour promised to be a new challenge for Lance. Tour officials didn't like how he had dominated in

兰斯在康复后担心癌症是否真的从他的体内消失了，他生活在癌症会回来的恐惧中。2001年10月，兰斯在取得环法比赛连续第3次胜利的几个月后，去了趟他的医生那里做检查。那时是他被诊断患有癌症的5周年——这对一个癌症幸存者而言是个很关键的时刻。如果5年后癌症还没有复发，医生会认为病人彻底摆脱了癌症。兰斯从医生那里得到了这样的消息。癌症消失了，而且永远不可能再回来了。

11月有更多的好消息，基克生下了双胞胎女婴伊莎贝拉和格蕾丝。一切似乎都很完美。但3个小孩子和繁忙的自行车比赛日程使兰斯和基克很难找到属于他俩的时间。他们不再像以前那样讨论很多事情，他们都专注于各自的生活，因而开始疏远对方。

然而兰斯和队友走得更近了。美国邮政车队因为其成员所穿的蓝色车手衫而得到了“大蓝”的绰号。兰斯连续3次在环法比赛夺冠，从而使这支从前名不见经传的车队成了一支强队。队中充满了优秀的队友——这些车手知道作为一个团队一起工作需要什么，为了使领袖车手取得优势，他们愿意工作，愿意流汗。

他们对兰斯和车队的奉献精神在2002年环法比赛中再次显现。兰斯想成为环法比赛历史上第4位连续4次夺冠的车手。如果他能做到，他将成为顶尖车手——像雅克·安格帝、埃迪·墨克斯和米盖尔·安杜兰——中的一员。

2002年环法比赛对兰斯而言注定是一场新的挑战。赛事官员不喜欢兰斯在前面3届环法比赛中那样

[1] were wrapped up in 专心致志于

[2] powerhouse 强大的集团；强国；（体育）强队

the past three races. They felt the last few stages were too boring, since everyone already knew who would win. Officials wanted to make the final stages more exciting. They changed the course so that many tough climbs came at the end. Lance would need his team's help more than ever.

The race started out perfectly, with Lance winning the opening time trial. He didn't hold on to the yellow jersey, though, knowing better than to try to keep up with the sprinters. He would wait for the mountains to get the jersey back. Again, he just wanted to stay out of trouble early on.

But trouble found Lance. During stage 7, he was caught up in a small crash. A teammate was bumped from behind and lost his balance. As he went down, his handlebars[1] got caught in the spokes[2] of Lance's rear tire. The team needed more than a minute to get back up and racing. The accident dropped Lance from third place to eighth.

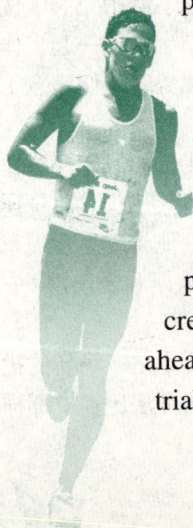

After a disappointing second-place finish in the stage 9 time trial, Lance came back in stage 11, a long and difficult climb over three peaks. Lance's teammates took turns leading him up the mountain, allowing him to draft and save energy. Finally, Lance was ready to attack. He rode at the front with Spain's Joseba Beloki, his main competition in the Tour. But he just couldn't leave the Spaniard behind. With about 200 meters (660 feet) to go, Lance made his move. Beloki couldn't keep up, and Lance crossed the finish line first, 7 seconds ahead. Lance had won the stage and took over the yellow jersey.

Big Blue kept pushing. The team seemed unstoppable in the mountains. Stage after stage, Lance increased his lead. Soon, he was four and a half minutes ahead of Beloki. Lance added a win at the stage 18 time trial and again cruised into Paris with victory.

主宰比赛。他们觉得最后几个赛段太乏味了，因为所有人已经知道谁会赢。官员们想让最后几个赛段更加刺激，他们修改了比赛路线，这样许多艰难的路段就被移到了比赛末尾。兰斯比任何时候都需要车队的帮助。

比赛开局很顺利，兰斯赢下了作为开幕赛的计时赛。但他并没有保住黄色领骑衫，他知道不应该和速度型选手硬拼。他会等到进入山区后再夺回黄色领骑衫。一如既往，他不想在比赛开始阶段找麻烦。

但麻烦找到了兰斯。在第7赛段，他卷入了一场小规模的撞车事故。一个队友被后面的车撞了一下，从而失去了平衡。当他摔倒时，他的自行车把手卡在了兰斯自行车后轮的辐条里。整个车队用了超过1分钟的时间才重新投入比赛。这次事故使兰斯的总成绩从第3名降到了第8名。

[1] handlebars （自行车等的）把手

[2] spokes 辐条；轮辐

在第9赛段的计时赛中，兰斯取得了令人失望的第2名，然后他在第11赛段卷土重来，这个长而艰苦的爬坡赛段横跨3座山。爬山时兰斯的队友轮流骑在他前面，让他“搭顺风车”以节省体力。最后，兰斯准备好冲刺了。他和他环法比赛中的主要对手——西班牙的何塞巴·贝洛基——都骑在前面。但他就是甩不开这个西班牙人。赛段还剩200米（660英尺）时，兰斯冲刺了。贝洛基跟不上，兰斯以领先7秒的成绩第一个冲过终点线。兰斯赢下了这个赛段，夺回了黄色领骑衫。

“大蓝”继续前进。这支车队在山区显得不可阻挡。一个又一个赛段过去了，兰斯扩大着自己的领先优势。很快，他就领先贝洛基4分30秒。兰斯在第18赛段的计时赛中又赢得胜利，再一次胜利挺进巴黎。

By tradition, the Tour winner gives a big chunk of his winnings (totaling about $400,000) to his teammates. Lance was so grateful for all the help he'd been given that he doubled the usual amount. He wanted to keep his teammates happy and make sure they stayed with the team. He was already thinking about a fifth-straight title in 2003.

Lance Armstrong's name was bigger than ever, and he continued to use it to call attention to the fight against cancer. At the end of 2002, he received one of the highest honors in sports when the magazine *Sports Illustrated* named him Sportsman of the Year.

Lance kept training hard. But as he did, the problems in his marriage grew. In February 2003, he and Kik separated. They wanted to spend some time apart to think about their marriage. It was a tough step. But because cyclists are often separated from their families, Lance was used to living on his own. He missed Kik and the children, but he threw his full attention into his training.

As the 2003 Tour approached, Lance had a streak[1] of bad luck. During a warm-up race, the thirty-one-year-old Lance crashed and hurt his hip. The week before the Tour, he got sick. A day before the race started, he still wasn't feeling well. In the Prologue, he finished a disappointing seventh. In stage 1, he went down in a crash, which left him with scrapes[2] and bruises. He had to borrow a teammate's bike to finish the stage.

Fans and other riders began to wonder if age had finally caught up with Lance Armstrong. Were his best racing days behind him? Was this the year his reign as champion would end? Jan Ullrich and others were eager to find out.

Throughout the early stages, Lance and his teammates used the same strategy they used every year—they just wanted to stay close to the leaders. They fought through

依照传统，环法比赛冠军会把比赛奖金（总额大约为40万美元）的一大部分分给队友。兰斯非常感激队友给他的帮助，所以他分给队友的钱是通常数额的两倍。他想让队友高兴，确保他们留在队里。他已经开始想在2003年取得五连冠了。

兰斯·阿姆斯特朗的名气比以往任何时候都要响，他继续利用自己的名声号召大家关注与癌症的斗争。2002年末，他接受了体育界的最高荣誉之一——《体育画报》杂志评选的年度最佳运动员。

兰斯继续刻苦训练，但与此同时，他的婚姻问题越来越严重。2003年2月，他和基克分居了。他们想分开一段时间，考虑他们的婚姻。这个过程很艰苦。但是因为自行车手经常和家庭分开，兰斯习惯了自己生活。他想念基克和孩子们，但他将全部注意力都投入到了训练中。

随着2003年环法比赛临近，兰斯霉运不断。在一次热身赛中，31岁的兰斯发生撞车事故，伤了臀部。环法比赛前一周，他生病了。比赛开始前一天，他还是感觉不舒服。在开幕赛中，他取得了令人失望的第7名。在第1赛段，他在撞车事故中摔倒，身上留下了擦伤和淤伤，他不得不借队友的自行车完成了这个赛段。

车迷和其他车手开始怀疑是否年龄最终开始对兰斯·阿姆斯特朗产生影响。他最好的比赛时间已经过去了？今年是他连续夺冠的终结？扬·乌尔里希和其他车手急切地想知道答案。

在比赛的整个开始阶段，兰斯和队友使用他们每年都使用的相同策略——紧跟着领先车手。他们

[1] streak　一连串，一系列

[2] scrapes　擦痕，擦伤

very hot weather and long, flat courses, waiting for the mountain stages. One highlight[1] for the team was winning stage 4, the team time trial. During this event, team members ride as a group. Everyone on the team earns the same time for the stage. U.S. Postal had often struggled in the event in past years.

Stage 8 was the first major climb into the Alps. In earlier years, Lance had dominated this part of the race. But this time he struggled with fatigue[2], and his opponents saw an opening. Finally, more than halfway through the 219-kilometer (136-mile) stage, Lance realized why he was so tired. His back brake was rubbing against the wheel. He was riding uphill with his brake on!

Lance fixed the problem and picked up speed. But his fourth-place finish was a disappointment, even though it was fast enough to give him the yellow jersey. Of bigger concern was his energy level. How much had all that extra work pedaling with the brake on cost his body? Only time would tell.

Lance had another scare in the next stage. Joseba Beloki, who started the day in second place, crashed while trying to make a turn. To avoid running into Beloki, Lance had to steer off the road. He didn't know what was waiting off the road. It could have been a cliff or a big rock. But he was lucky—he sailed into an open field. He kept going, pedaling through the field, looking for a place to get back on the road. But before he could do so, he came upon a big ditch[3]. He had to carry his bike over it. Finally, he got back on the road and hurried to catch up with the leaders. Beloki was not as lucky. He suffered several broken bones and had to withdraw from the race.

In the stage 12 time trial, Lance had more problems. He ran out of water on a brutally hot day. Tour rules don't

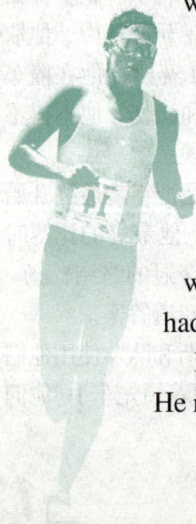

冒着高温，在长而平坦的赛道上拼搏，等待着山区赛段。其中最激动人心的事情是车队赢下了第4赛段，这是一个团体计时赛。比赛中，车队队员们作为一个集体骑行，每位队员本赛段的比赛成绩完全一样。美国邮政车队往年在这项比赛中都很吃力。

第8赛段是进入阿尔卑斯山的第一个重要爬坡赛段。前几年兰斯都主宰着这个赛段，但这次，疲劳使他在比赛中很吃力，他的对手看到有机可乘。最后，219公里（136英里）长的比赛进行了一大半时，兰斯意识到他如此疲劳的原因。他的自行车的后刹车正在摩擦着车轮。他一直带着刹车在爬坡！

兰斯处理了这个问题，提高了速度。但他取得了令人失望的第4名，即使这已经足够他赢得黄色领骑衫。更为重要的是他的体力问题。带着刹车骑车总共额外消耗了多少体力？只有时间能给出答案。

在下一个赛段中，兰斯又遇上了可怕的事情。当天第2个出发的何塞巴·贝洛基在试图转弯时摔倒。为了避免撞上贝洛基，兰斯不得不骑车离开公路。他不知道公路旁是什么，有可能是悬崖，也有可能是巨大的岩石。但他很幸运——他骑到了一片空地上。他继续前进，踩着踏板穿越空地，寻找重新回到公路上的地方。但还没有找到，他就碰上了一个大沟，他不得不背着自行车过了沟。最终他回到了公路上，加速赶上前面的领先选手。贝洛基没有这么幸运，他摔断了几根骨头，不得不退出比赛。

在第12赛段的计时赛中，兰斯遇到了更多问题。天气酷热，他的水用完了。比赛规则规定

[1] highlight　最精彩的部分；最重要的事情

[2] fatigue　疲劳

[3] ditch　沟，水渠

allow riders to get any help during time trials, so no one could give Lance the drink he badly needed. Ullrich, still Lance's biggest rival for the championship, gained more than a minute and a half during the 47-kilometer (29-mile) stage.

"I had an incredible crisis," Lance said after the stage. "I felt like I was pedaling backward." And although Lance held on to the yellow jersey with a slim lead, Ullrich had more reason than ever to believe that Lance's Tour dominance might be over.

Lance struggled again in stage 13. His body had lost a lot of water, and he still hadn't fully recovered. Ullrich closed in[1], pulling within 15 seconds of the overall lead. But despite everything that had gone wrong, Lance was still wearing the yellow jersey at the end of the stage.

After Lance and Ullrich finished stage 14 side by side, the lead was still 15 seconds. By then, Lance was feeling better. He knew that only a few stages remained. He needed to make a move before the race left the mountains.

But Ullrich was confident. He'd seen Lance at his worst and told the media that he'd have the lead by the end of stage 15. The comments motivated Lance. He set off to win the stage and build the kind of comfortable lead he was used to.

Early in the stage, Ullrich made an attack. Lance didn't try to go with him, though, knowing how much more riding was to come. Lance was right—Ullrich couldn't keep up the speed, and the lead group quickly caught back up to him.

As the cyclists reached the final climb of the stage, Lance saw that Ullrich had dropped behind the pack. He'd worn himself out with the early attack. Lance saw his opportunity. He stood up on his pedals and charged. He was pulling away. He thought he would take control of the

在计时赛中车手不能得到任何帮助，因此没人能提供兰斯急需的饮用水。乌尔里希依然是兰斯夺冠的最大对手，他在这个47公里（29英里）长的赛段中领先超过1分30秒。

兰斯在赛段结束后说："我遭遇了可怕的危机，我感觉好像在往后骑。"尽管兰斯以微弱的优势保住了黄色领骑衫，乌尔里希比以往更有理由相信，兰斯主宰环法比赛的日子可能要结束了。

在第13赛段，兰斯依然很吃力。他的身体失去了大量水分，并且他还没有完全恢复过来。乌尔里希追赶上来，把自己与兰斯在总成绩上的差距缩短到15秒内。但是尽管出了这么多问题，兰斯在赛段结束后依然保有黄色领骑衫。

[1] closed in 逼近，围上来

兰斯与乌尔里希肩并肩完成了第14赛段后，兰斯的领先优势依然是15秒。这时兰斯感觉好些了。他知道只剩下几个赛段，他必须在离开山区前有所行动。

但乌尔里希充满自信。他看到了处于最糟糕状态的兰斯，他告诉媒体，他将在第15赛段结束前取得领先。这样的言论刺激了兰斯，他要赢下这个赛段，并且确立他已经习惯了的那种绰绰有余的领先优势。

在赛段开始阶段，乌尔里希开始冲刺。但兰斯并没有跟着冲刺，因为他知道路途还很漫长。兰斯是对的——乌尔里希不能一直保持高速度，领先的车群很快就重新赶上了他。

当车手们到达赛段最后一个坡路时，兰斯看到乌尔里希已经落在了车群后面，他因为过早冲刺而筋疲力尽。兰斯看到自己的机会来了，他站在踏板上冲刺，甩开了车群。他想他可以重新控

Tour again and leave all his bad luck behind.

As he attacked, he saw a fan in front of him. The young boy was swinging a yellow bag. By the time Lance saw the danger, it was too late. The bag caught his handlebar. In an instant, Lance was falling over sideways, smashing his right side on the pavement and scraping his elbow. For a moment, he thought he might be seriously injured. His hip hurt. He briefly wondered if he'd be able to continue or whether this was how his quest[1] for a fifth championship would end.

He wasn't going to go down that easily, though. He got up and jumped back on his bike. "After the fall, I had a big, big rush of adrenaline[2]," he said.

After a few minutes, he was ready to resume[3] his attack. Again, he pulled away. Ullrich and the other riders simply couldn't keep up with the furious climb. Lance crossed the finish line alone. He had extended his lead over Ullrich to 1:07 with five stages to go. But bleeding and exhausted, he didn't even celebrate his stage win. "This has been a Tour of too many problems, too many close calls," he said. "I wish it would stop. I wish I could just have some uneventful[4] days."

For the next three stages, Lance and Ullrich rode together, neither able to gain much time. With two stages left, Lance's lead was 1:05. Stage 19 would be the key. Ullrich had to gain a big chunk of time to have any chance entering the final stage. But as hard as he tried, Ullrich couldn't cut into the lead. In fact, Lance added another 11 seconds to the margin, pretty much assuring himself another title.

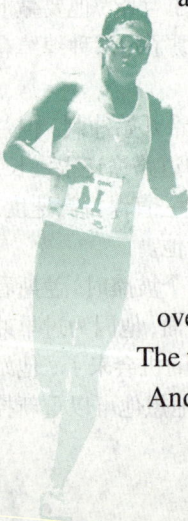

When no disasters came in stage 20, the race was over. Lance Armstrong had again won the Tour de France. The title was his fifth, tying him with four others—Jacques Anquetil, Eddy Merckx, Bernard Hinault, and Miguel

制环法比赛，把所有的霉运抛到脑后。

他在冲刺时，看到前面有一个车迷，这个小男孩在挥舞着一个黄色袋子。兰斯发现危险的时候，已经太晚了。袋子勾住了他的自行车把手。兰斯立刻向边上摔去，整个右边身体摔在地上，肘部擦伤了。有那么一会儿，他觉得自己可能伤得很重。他的臀部很疼。他稍稍怀疑了一下自己是否还能继续比赛，是否他第5次夺冠的追求就将这样结束。

[1] quest 追求；探索

但是他不会这么轻易地倒下。他站起来，跳上自行车。他说："倒地后，我感觉肾上腺素大量分泌。"

[2] adrenaline 肾上腺素

几分钟后，他准备好再次冲刺。他又一次甩开了对手。乌尔里希和其他车手完全不能跟上他爬坡的速度。兰斯独自冲过终点线。比赛还剩下5个赛段，他对乌尔里希的领先优势扩大到了1分7秒。但还在流血、筋疲力尽的兰斯甚至没有庆祝这个赛段的胜利。他说："这次环法比赛出现了太多问题和太多千钧一发的时刻。我希望这些不幸不再发生。我希望能够风平浪静地度过几天。"

[3] resume 重新开始；继续

[4] uneventful 平静无事的

在接下来的3个赛段中，兰斯和乌尔里希齐头并进，谁也无法领先很多时间。当比赛还剩下两个赛段时，兰斯的领先优势是1分5秒。第19赛段将是关键。乌尔里希想要在进入最后一个赛段时还有机会的话，就必须取得很大的领先优势。但无论乌尔里希如何努力，他就是无法缩短他和兰斯之间的差距。事实上，兰斯又把领先优势扩大了11秒，大大确保了又一次夺冠的可能性。

第20赛段没有事故发生，环法比赛结束了。兰斯·阿姆斯特朗再次赢得环法比赛冠军。他的第5次夺冠把他和其他4位车手联系在了一起——雅克·安格帝、埃迪·墨克斯、伯纳德·黑诺特和米盖尔·安杜兰——

Indurain—for the most Tour wins ever. Indurain was the only other rider to have won five in a row.

"It's a dream, really a dream," Lance said. "I love cycling, I love my job and I will be back for a sixth. It's incredible to win again."

这些都是在环法比赛中夺冠次数最多的车手。安杜兰是唯一另外一位取得五连冠的车手。

兰斯说:“这是场梦,真的是一场梦。我热爱自行车比赛,我喜欢我的工作,我将回来争取第6次夺冠。能再次夺冠真是不可思议。”

CHAPTER TEN

RECORD SETTER

创造纪录

After his 2003 Tour victory, Lance took some time away from cycling. He promoted his new book, *Every Second Counts*. He also took part in charity events, did interviews, and appeared on talk shows.

Lance and Kik also tried to get back together during this time. But by September, they decided that the marriage wasn't working and announced that they would divorce. Despite the breakup of their marriage, Lance and Kik remained friends. They lived near each other in Austin and shared custody[1] of their children.

Not long after the divorce, Lance had a new woman in his life. He began to date rock singer Sheryl Crow, whom he met at a charity event in Las Vegas. "We're very similar," Lance said. "She likes to stay busy. She's always on, and I like that....When we're together, we never feel bothered or uncomfortable."

Despite the changes in his personal life, Lance managed to focus on his only real goal for 2004—winning a record sixth Tour de France. Nobody had ever done it. He was excited to be going back to France with his U.S. Postal Service team.

In the Prologue, Lance finished second to Switzerland's Fabian Cancellara. But he finished 15 seconds ahead of Jan Ullrich and his other main challengers. Rain and bad weather followed the Tour throughout the early stages, so more than ever, Lance's goal was just to stay out of trouble. He dropped several places in the standings, but he wasn't worried.

Stage 4 was the team time trial. After winning this event in 2003, Lance's team had high hopes. A steady rain had

2003年在环法比赛中夺冠后，兰斯离开了自行车比赛一段时间。他为他的新书《分秒必争》做宣传。他还参加了一些慈善活动，接受采访，并出现在电视谈话节目中。

兰斯和基克在这段时间中也努力想要重新生活在一起。但到了9月，他们认定婚姻无法维持下去，并宣布将要离婚。尽管婚姻破裂了，兰斯和基克还是朋友。他们在奥斯丁住得很近，共同拥有对孩子的监护权。

[1] custody 监护（权）

离婚后不久，兰斯的生活中又有了一个女人。他开始和摇滚歌星谢丽尔·克罗约会，他是在拉斯维加斯的一个慈善活动中遇到她的。兰斯说："我们非常像。她喜欢忙碌，她总是在忙，我很喜欢这点……当我们在一起时，从来不感到不安或不舒服。"

尽管兰斯的私生活发生变化，他还是努力把注意力放在他2004年唯一真正的目标上——打破纪录，第6次夺取环法比赛冠军。没有人曾经做到过。他很兴奋地与美国邮政车队回到法国。

开幕赛中，兰斯取得第2，输给了瑞士的法比安·坎塞拉拉。但他领先扬·乌尔里希和其他几位主要挑战者15秒。比赛开始阶段一直在下雨，天气很糟糕，因此兰斯的目标就是避免卷入麻烦，这个目标比以往更显得明确。他的总成绩排名下降了几位，但他并不担心。

第4赛段是团体计时赛。2003年，兰斯所在的车队赢下了这个赛段，因此期望很高。比

fallen for much of the day, but the weather finally let up as Big Blue was making its run. The combination of improved weather and good strategy gave the U.S. Postal Service team the win and helped Lance gain the yellow jersey for the first time in the 2004 Tour.

Other riders attacked early in stage 6, but Lance didn't try to chase them. The mountains were still a week away, and he didn't plan to hold the yellow jersey until then. He was content to finish back in the pack. He lost the lead and fell to sixth place, more than 9 minutes behind leader Thomas Voeckler.

Lance held that place over the next several stages, flat courses that favored sprinters. He stayed near Voeckler, riding and waiting. Entering stage 12, he was 9:35 back. But the mountains had come.

Heavy rains fell on the peloton as it entered the Pyrenees. It was perfect weather for Lance and his teammates, who were used to practicing in such conditions. On the final climb, they made a serious attack. Voeckler couldn't keep up. Their blistering[1] pace took its toll on many strong competitors, including Jan Ullrich and Lance's former teammate Tyler Hamilton.

Only Ivan Basso, an Italian rider and Lance's good friend, was able to keep up. Basso's mother was fighting cancer, and the two riders had formed a close bond[2]. As the two approached the stage's finish line, everyone expected Lance to make a mad sprint to the finish. But he didn't. He fell in behind Basso and took second place out of respect for his friend.

The two men were again side by side as they chased the stage 13 finish. They worked together to set a pace that their rivals couldn't maintain. But this time, Lance wasn't content with second. He sprinted to the finish for the win, his first stage victory of the 2004 Tour. The

赛那天一直在下雨，但当“大蓝”要出发时雨终于停了。有所好转的天气以及得当的策略使得美国邮政车队赢下了这个赛段，从而帮助兰斯在2004年环法比赛中第一次穿上黄色领骑衫。

其他选手在第6赛段中早早开始冲刺，但兰斯不想追上他们。还有一个星期才进入山地，他计划到那时再保有黄色领骑衫。落在车群后面完成比赛，他很满足。他失去领先位置，总成绩降到第6名，比领先车手托马斯·弗克勒落后超过9分钟。

兰斯在接下来几个对冲刺型选手有利的平地赛段中保持着第6的位置。他紧跟弗克勒骑行，等待着机会。进入第12赛段时，他落后9分35秒。但比赛进入到山地。

主车群进入比利牛斯山时，下起了暴雨。这种天气对习惯了在这种条件下练习的兰斯和队友来说非常有利。在最后一个坡路，他们急速冲刺。弗克勒跟不上。他们极快的速度对包括扬·乌尔里希和兰斯的前队友泰勒·汉密尔顿在内的很多强有力的对手施加了不利的影响。

只有兰斯的好友——意大利车手伊万·巴索——能够跟上。巴索的母亲在与癌症抗争，这两个车手关系很亲近。当他们接近赛段终点线时，所有人都预料兰斯会疯狂冲刺到终点。但是他没有。出于对朋友的尊重，他落在巴索后面，取得了第2名。

当快到第13赛段终点时，又是这两人并驾齐驱。他们一起协作，把速度提高到他们的对手都无法保持的程度。但这次，兰斯不满足于第2名。他冲刺到终点，第一次赢得了2004年环法比赛的赛段胜利。这次胜利使他的总成绩排名提前到

[1] blistering （速度等）极快的

[2] bond （感情、利益等上的）联系

win moved him into second place overall, 22 seconds behind Voeckler. Basso was third, 1:39 back.

Lance's next move came in stage 15. Voeckler fell back with a flat tire. Lance knew this was his chance to take back control of the race. With a burst of energy at the end, Lance barely beat Basso and Ullrich for the stage win. More important, he had the yellow jersey back with a lead of 1:25 over Basso.

Lance and his teammates were happy to have the lead, but they were also worried. Basso was riding well. Lance didn't have much margin for error. A minute and a half just wasn't a comfortable lead.

Stage 16 was a time trial—Lance's best chance to extend his lead. Basso wasn't strong in time trials, while Lance had always excelled there. Sure enough, Lance took advantage of the opportunity. He was the last to start, 2 minutes after Basso. Lance caught the Italian with about 3 kilometers (1.9 miles) to go. He won the stage by more than a minute over Ullrich and increased his overall lead to 3:48 over Basso. With four stages left, Lance's pursuit of a record sixth-straight victory seemed almost assured.

But Lance wasn't done dominating the race. He won again the next day, the 204-kilometer (127-mile) climb of stage 17. Then he won again in stage 19, the final time trial. Lance had another huge lead entering the final stage and crossed the finish line without much drama. He had done what no other cyclist had ever done—he'd won six Tours. He'd also set another record. At age thirty-two, he was the oldest winner in the race's history.

As he stood on the podium after the race, "The Star-Spangled Banner" played over the loudspeakers. The next song was "All I Wanna Do (Is Have Some Fun)," one of Sheryl Crow's biggest hits.

第2位，比弗克勒落后22秒。巴索排在第3，落后1分39秒。

兰斯在第15赛段采取了下一步行动。弗克勒因爆胎而落后。兰斯知道这是他重新控制比赛的机会。凭借赛段末的突然发力，兰斯险胜巴索和乌尔里希，夺得赛段胜利。更重要的是，他夺回了黄色领骑衫，领先巴索1分25秒。

拥有了领先位置，兰斯和队友很高兴，但他们也很担心。巴索状态很好，兰斯的领先优势不大，不容犯错。1分半钟并不是很大的领先优势。

第16赛段是个计时赛——兰斯最好的扩大领先优势的机会。巴索在计时赛中能力不强，而兰斯总是表现出色。毫无疑问，兰斯利用了这个机会。他最后一个出发，比巴索晚2分钟。比赛还剩大约3公里（1.9英里）时，兰斯赶上了这个意大利人。他以领先乌尔里希超过1分钟的优势赢下了这个赛段，总成绩上对巴索的领先优势扩大到3分48秒。比赛还剩下4个赛段，兰斯对于创纪录的六连冠的追求看起来几乎要成功了。

但兰斯对比赛的主宰还没有结束。兰斯又赢下了第2天进行的第17赛段，这是个长204公里（127英里）的爬坡赛段。然后他又赢了第19赛段，这也是最后一个计时赛。进入最后一个赛段时，兰斯又一次取得了巨大的领先优势，毫无悬念地冲过了比赛终点线。他取得了其他车手从未取得过的成绩——他6次夺取了环法比赛的冠军。他也创下了又一个纪录：32岁的他是赛事历史上年纪最大的冠军。

当他赛后站在领奖台上时，喇叭里播放着美国国歌《星条旗永不落》。下一首歌是谢丽尔·克罗的热门歌曲之一——《我想做的是（找一点乐子）》。

Lance enjoyed the victory with his teammates, knowing the next year would be one of change. It was the last time Lance would wear his U.S. Postal Service jersey. The team's sponsorship was changing. The Discovery Channel was taking over as sponsor, although the team members remained the same.

Lance stayed in the headlines throughout the rest of 2004 and the early part of 2005. Nike and the Lance Armstrong Foundation started a new fund-raising effort called WEARYELLOW LIVESTRONG. The foundation sold yellow wristbands for $1 apiece to raise money for cancer research. The campaign, along with other fundraisers, raised $50 million in one year.

Lance also was in the headlines as his relationship with Sheryl grew. News photographers loved to take pictures of the famous couple. And Lance still could not escape doping rumors.

As the 2005 Tour approached, reporters wanted to know Lance's future plans. Finally, on April 18, 2005, Lance made a statement. "I have decided the [2005] Tour de France will be my last race as a professional cyclist," he said. "Ultimately, athletes have to retire...the body doesn't just keep going and going."

Lance already had the record. His name was forever sealed as one of the greatest cyclists in history. Whether he finished first, last, or anywhere in between in the 2005 Tour wouldn't change that. But Lance wanted to go out as a winner. He wanted his final race to be a celebration of his whole career. The only way to do that was to win.

As always, Lance and his teammates trained hard. Nothing less than victory would be acceptable. As he had for years, he treated many of the spring races as tune-ups[1]. His vision was focused on that final Tour. Finally, July

兰斯和队友一起享受比赛的胜利，他们知道下一年会出现变化。这是兰斯最后一次身穿美国邮政车队的车手服。虽然车队成员不变，但车队的赞助商换了，探索频道成为赞助商。

在2004年余下的时间里和2005年初，兰斯始终出现在头条新闻中。耐克和兰斯·阿姆斯特朗基金会发起了新的名为“戴黄腕带，坚强生活”的筹款活动。基金会通过出售价格为1美元的黄腕带来为癌症研究筹款。这次活动和其他筹款活动在一年里筹集了5 000万美元。

兰斯也因为和谢丽尔的恋情发展而登上头条。新闻摄影记者热衷于拍摄这对著名情侣的照片。而且兰斯依然摆脱不了有关他服药的谣言。

随着2005年环法比赛临近，记者想知道兰斯未来的计划。最终在2005年4月18日，兰斯发表了声明：“我已经决定（2005年）环法比赛将是我作为职业自行车手的最后一场比赛。运动员最终都要退役……身体不可能一直在高强度运转。”

兰斯已经创造了纪录。他将作为最伟大的自行车手之一而永载史册。无论他在2005年环法比赛中取得第一名，还是最后一名，抑或是其他名次，都无法改变这一点。但兰斯想作为冠军退出自行车界。他想让自己的最后一场比赛成为他整个职业生涯的庆祝仪式。要做到这一点只有夺冠。

兰斯和队友一如既往地刻苦训练。除了冠军，其他都不可接受。像往年一样，他把很多春季赛事当做调整的机会。他的视线集中在最终的环法比赛上。7月终于到来。兰斯最

[1] tune-ups　热身活动；调节

came. Lance made his last trip to France as a competitor. All the attention was focused on him as he sat on his bike before the Prologue, the last of 189 riders, waiting for his signal to start.

But his quest for a seventh Tour championship started with a sputter[1]. His foot slipped off his pedal. He quickly got it back on and took off riding. Before long, he had Jan Ullrich (who had started a minute earlier) in sight. He passed the German and cruised to a second-place finish. His lead over Ullrich was 1:06.

Lance used his usual early-race strategy by riding with the pack and staying out of trouble. The Discovery Channel team won the team time trial in stage 4. But in stage 8, the first stage in the mountains, where Lance liked to turn up the heat, he found himself in real trouble. A group of riders set a blistering pace, determined to isolate the thirty-three-year-old American. The plan worked—Lance's teammates couldn't keep up the pace. Soon, he was alone, without any help.

Lance kept fighting, though. He couldn't win the stage, but he managed to finish in a pack only 27 seconds behind the leaders. The day had taken a heavy toll on his legs, and he'd missed the opportunity to take control of the race. But he'd survived.

Only two stages later, Lance had a new chance to take control. Stage 10 was the first of several brutal climbs—exactly the sort of stage Lance could use to build a huge lead on his rivals. This time, there were no mistakes. He made a big attack that Jan Ullrich, Ivan Basso, and the other competitors couldn't match. He finished the stage second, with an overall lead of 38 seconds over Mickael Rasmussen.

As the stages passed by, the lead slowly grew. By the end of stage 19, his lead was 2:46 over Basso. With only two stages to go, it was a very comfortable lead. But

后一次作为选手来到法国。在开幕赛开始前，他坐在自行车上等待比赛开始的信号时，所有的注意力都集中到了他身上，他在189名选手中排在最后一位。

[1] sputter 劈啪声；喷溅出的（食物等）

但他冲击第7次环法比赛冠军的努力在开始时却遇到个小麻烦。他的脚从脚踏板上滑了下来。他迅速重新踩上脚踏板并开始骑行。很快他看到了扬·乌尔里希（比兰斯早1分钟出发）。他超过了这个德国人，以第2名的成绩冲过终点线。他领先乌尔里希1分6秒。

兰斯采用了他比赛前段惯常使用的策略：跟着车群，避开麻烦。探索频道车队赢下了第4赛段的团体计时赛。但在第8赛段——第一个山地赛段，他遇到了真正的麻烦，而以前他总喜欢在这里加快速度。一组车手把速度提得很高，决心孤立这个33岁的美国人。他们的计划奏效了——兰斯的队友无法维持这样快的速度。很快，兰斯就孤军奋战了。

但兰斯继续战斗。他没有赢下这个赛段，但他成功地与另外一组车手一起完成了比赛，只比领先的车手们慢了27秒。那天的比赛对他的腿部产生了非常不利的影响，他错过了控制比赛的机会。但是他挺了过来。

仅仅两个赛段之后，兰斯又有一个控制比赛的机会。第10赛段是几个严酷的爬坡赛段中的第一个——这正是兰斯可以加以利用从而大大领先对手的那种赛段。这一次没出什么差错。他发起猛烈冲刺，扬·乌尔里希、伊万·巴索和其他对手都无法跟上。他以第2名的成绩完成这个赛段，总成绩比迈克尔·拉斯姆森领先了38秒。

随着比赛的进行，他的领先优势慢慢地扩大。第19赛段结束时，他领先巴索2分46秒。比赛还剩下两个赛段，这是绰绰有余的领先优势。但还

something was missing. Not counting the team time trial, Lance still hadn't won a stage. He wanted to change that with the stage 20 time trial—the last time trial in his amazing career.

Lance rode with purpose. He went hard and blew the field away on the 55-kilometer (34-mile) course. When he crossed the finish line, he'd won the stage by 23 seconds over Ullrich and increased his overall lead to more than 4 minutes.

Stage 21 marked the end of the Tour and the last ride of Lance's professional career. Because of severe weather, officials declared Lance the winner with about 48 kilometers (30 miles) still to go. For Lance, the ride into Paris was a long victory parade. As he crossed the finish line, his career as a professional cyclist ended. Lance Armstrong had won his seventh-straight Tour de France, a feat that might never be matched.

"It's nice to finish your career on a high note," Lance had said the day before, knowing that his Tour victory was assured. "As a sportsman, I wanted to go out on top."

少点什么。除了团体计时赛以外，兰斯还没有赢下一个赛段。他想在第20赛段的计时赛中改变这一点——这是他辉煌的职业生涯中最后一个计时赛。

兰斯带着这个目的比赛。他在55公里（34英里）长的赛道上快速骑行，大败全场所有选手。当他冲过终点线时，他以领先乌尔里希23秒的成绩赢下了这个赛段，把总成绩的领先优势扩大到超过4分钟。

第21赛段标志着环法比赛的结束，同时也是兰斯职业生涯的结束。因为恶劣的天气，赛事官员在比赛还剩下48公里（30英里）时宣布兰斯夺冠。对兰斯而言，进入巴黎的路段是一段长距离的胜利游行。当他冲过终点线时，他的职业自行车手生涯结束了。兰斯·阿姆斯特朗连续第7次夺得环法自行车赛冠军，这样的丰功伟绩可能永远无人能比肩。

知道自己胜利在握的兰斯在比赛结束前一天曾说:“能在巅峰时结束自己的职业生涯非常美妙。作为一个运动员，我想在巅峰时退出。”

EPILOGUE
尾声

MOVING ON
继续前进

After Lance's victory in the 2005 Tour de France, he stood on the podium with his three children. The crowd cheered. His son, Luke, looked uncomfortable in front of all the people. He asked Lance if they could go home.

For once, Lance could finally answer yes. He was ready to go home. He was eager to go back to Texas and be a dad. He also looked forward to more time with Sheryl. In September 2005, he proposed to her, and she agreed to marry him.

A few months later, Lance and Sheryl called off[1] their engagement. They said they continued to have great respect for each other, and it was a difficult decision for both of them. Fortunately for Lance, he had some happier news to focus on—he had been named Associated Press Male Athlete of the Year for the fourth-straight year. It was one more record-setting accomplishment for the newly retired cyclist.

Lance's retirement allowed him to do more work with the Lance Armstrong Foundation and the LIVESTRONG program, which had sold more than 50 million wristbands. He also had time for new activities. He talked about possibly running for political office someday.

Asked if he would ever consider a return to cycling to chase yet another Tour victory, Lance said, "Now that we have number seven, number eight doesn't really make a difference. It's time for me to move on with my life."

Lance planned to keep working with his old team, consulting with coaches and riders, helping them build a new identity and a new winning tradition. At the same time, he looked forward to leaving the intense world of

兰斯在2005年环法比赛中夺冠后，与他的3个子女一起站在了领奖台上。观众们在欢呼。他的儿子卢克在这么多人面前很不适应，他问兰斯他们是否能回家。

这一次，兰斯终于能回答“是的”。他准备好回家了。他急切地想回到得克萨斯，急切地想做一个爸爸。他也盼望着和谢丽尔待在一起的时间更长。2005年9月，他向她求婚，她同意嫁给他。

[1] called off 取消

几个月后，兰斯和谢丽尔取消了他们的订婚。他们说他们仍然非常尊重对方，做出这样的决定对他们双方都很困难。还好对兰斯而言，他收到一些更让人高兴的消息——他连续第4年被评选为美联社年度最佳男运动员。对于这个刚刚退役的自行车手而言，这是又一个创纪录的成就。

退役后，兰斯能为兰斯·阿姆斯特朗基金会和已经售出超过5 000万个腕带的“坚强生活”活动做更多的工作。他也有时间从事新的活动。他谈到有一天可能会从政。

当被问到是否会考虑回到自行车赛场去争取另一个环法比赛胜利时，兰斯说：“既然我们已经有了7个，那第8个就并没有什么区别了。现在是继续我的生活的时候了。”

兰斯计划继续和原来的车队共同工作，为教练和车手提供建议，帮助他们确立车队新的特点和新的获胜传统。同时，他也盼望着离开竞争激

professional cycling behind for a little while.

But the cycling world wasn't ready to leave Lance behind. In August 2005, new rumors surfaced[1] about Lance and drug use. In a French newspaper story, reporters claimed to have proof that Lance had used a performance-enhancing drug called EPO during the 1999 Tour.

Lance's response was the same as it had always been. He told reporters that he'd never used performance-enhancing drugs. He called the newspaper story a "witch hunt[2]." The rumors angered Lance so much that he even talked about returning for the 2006 Tour de France, just to prove himself all over again.

Despite drug use rumors, it's doubtful that anything could ever hurt Lance Armstrong's legacy. He was a young, brash American in a sport dominated by Europeans. He was forgotten, beaten by cancer, and cast aside. But he never gave up on himself. Through sheer[3] determination and will, he made himself into the greatest cyclist the world has ever known. It's possible that one day his record will be matched or broken, but his inspirational story—probably the greatest comeback story in sports history—will never be topped.

烈的职业自行车界一小段时间。

但自行车界并不准备离开兰斯。2005年8月，关于兰斯服药的新谣言出现了。在一家法国报纸的一篇报道中，记者声称有证据证明兰斯在1999年的环法比赛中使用了一种名为EPO的提高比赛成绩的药物。

兰斯的反应一如既往。他告诉记者他从未使用过提高比赛成绩的药物。他把那篇新闻报道称为“政治迫害”。谣言激怒了兰斯，他甚至说要重返2006年环法比赛，就为了再一次证明自己。

尽管有这些服药的传闻，但并没有什么东西能够贬低兰斯·阿姆斯特朗留下的遗产。他是在欧洲人主宰的一项体育项目中一个年轻而又咄咄逼人的美国人。他曾被遗忘，曾被癌症侵袭，曾被抛在一边。但他从来没有放弃自己。凭借坚强的决心和意志，他使自己成为世界上最好的自行车手。可能有一天他的纪录将被追平或打破，但他鼓舞人心的故事——这可能是体育史上最伟大的重返赛场的故事——将永远无法被超越。

[1] surfaced 显露；浮出水面

[2] witch hunt 政治迫害

[3] sheer 完美的，十足的；彻底的